7-18

Switching Heads

by

Tom Sullivan

D1452409

DORRANCE PUBLISHING CO., INC.
PITTSBURGH, PENNSYLVANIA 15222

ISBN: 978-1-4349-0471-3
Printed in the United States of America

First Printing

For information or to order additional books, please write:
Dorrance Publishing Co., Inc.
701 Smithfield St.
Pittsburgh, Pennsylvania 15222
U.S.A.
1-800-788-7654
www.dorrancebookstore.com

Thank you to my family, friends, and Dr G for all your
help and support

INTRODUCTION

As we grow older and realize the mortality of our situation here on earth, we from time to time may think about our own death. It is not something that folks like to dwell on, even for a passing moment. There are many uncertainties about dying. Imagine as a young child you are thrust into a situation where death surrounds you at every turn. Its constant presence in your thinking becomes a torturous reminder of what can happen at any moment.

Many friends have encouraged me to write this story. It seems I may have procrastinated for reasons that may be clearer when you are done reading. I once read—it may have been Andy Rooney who said it—that 80 percent of all Americans believe that their story was one that, if they had the time to write it, would be a best seller. While I believe Andy's observation, I also have thought long and hard about what makes this story different, and I have moved forward with the project.

I never really had the time or the inclination to think if my story was different or not. Over the years, as I have spoken to different people and shared some of the things that are described in this book, the response I typically have received is that "those" stories are gross and "I don't know how you sleep at night." The stories are indeed gruesome, and, until recently, I did not sleep well at all. Death dreams were a constant companion from age twenty.

It is important to understand that, as I contemplated the content of the story, it was not so much the fact that what I had lived and observed was fact, or amazing; it was that it was being seen through the eyes of a ten-year-old. Looking back on the experiences, and now looking at my own daughters, it seems to me maddening that I was exposed to these situations at such an early age.

The youthful observation and its impact, combined with what now looks like a combination of *CSI* and *Night of the Living Dead*, made me believe that not only would the story have merit but also that some valuable lessons could be learned. Death can be a respected ritual in many cultures. I'm not sure my intention is to expose any bad behaviors in one religion over another. Our belief system about death and what happens in the afterlife are not topics here. The story here is much simpler. As I grew older, my memories would not calm. I needed to be free of those thoughts. Much work, smart doctors, spiritual guidance, and good medication have all helped quell the visions that played over and over.

My insight tells me that seeing the situations described was at some level a very interesting opportunity. It gave me insight into what I should respect in life, and it taught me how to stay alive, although it seemed I often forgot that aspect. I recall vividly walking past the yellow tape surrounding crime scenes on a regular basis. As I said, there was something cool about having the ability to go over that tape and not get yelled at by the many police in the area.

When someone dies at home of natural causes, the tape is not necessary, but if you get your head blown off, the place will be taped off. Even back in those days, the effort to maintain a clean crime scene was evident, although when I think of the night spent with the List family, the place seemed to be crawling with all kinds of people—police captains, chief detectives, EMTs, doctors, photographers, and, of course, myself. This played over and over again. I became a familiar face to many of the police who were lucky enough to have shared witness to some of the scenes.

I recall car wrecks very well—remember the type of car and the condition of the body. When you pick up at the scene, that is when it is the most explicit. Someone still in the car or near the car. Usually soaked in blood with broken bones. By the time we get them back to the home, the optics are not the same. I think it is the car still being in the picture. The awkward feeling you have when you are standing in the third lane of the Parkway. It feels like you should not be there. Of course the traffic is stopped, but it still feels strange. People usually do not stand in this lane…at any time.

Some of the story is graphic. These descriptions are not gratuitous. My recollections are as if some happened yesterday. Others are less clear but are used to be illustrative of what I was living and seeing on a daily basis.

The bottom line was that I was exposed to many things at an early age that we would not think of exposing a kid to in today's nanny-filled world.

Some memories are quite graphic. The emotional scars that some of these memories had on me are striking and memorable. It supports the theory that if you do something—anything—long enough, you will grow frighteningly accustomed to some very nontraditional sights and sounds.

Graphic scenes are no longer as shocking as they were at one time. Keep in mind the backdrop of this story, 1967–1982, when news coverage was not as ugly or as available as it is today.

There is also some humor, as inappropriate as some may find it, throughout the story. My dad was a funny guy, and I believe he used his sense of humor to cover up the pain that was in his job. He was a pretty deep guy and at the same time kept a pretty even keel most of the time.

We need to understand that both my parents were big-league drinkers. Many of the stories in here mention drinking. Alcohol was a big part of my family's life and became a big part of my life as well. Drinking at a funeral was not necessarily a bad thing—a shot to calm the nerves.

In my case, by a strange coincidence, I began drinking around the time I was ten years old. This was the same time we moved into the funeral home. I always believed the connection between the funeral business and my behavior was strong. I surmised I saw bad stuff and did not want to face them. I obviously did not see this as it was happening. That would be too easy.

The events described here are not meant to disrespect anyone. Some are just funny, and others were funny moments that happened at bad times.

It seems like death, as a topic, ebbs and flows in our society today. It never really becomes a topic in and of itself but is always related to some event. John Lennon and Tim Russert, come to mind. We never really celebrate death the way some cultures do.

Death has become less taboo these days. *Six Feet Under*, *CSI*, and a collection of books that claim to tell the story and illustrate what happens during death, after death, and around death are examples. I'm not really sure what happens after death. I do know what happens to you when you die here on earth. As you may suspect, it is not always pretty.

It always amazed me what one person would do to another. When you view the physical outcome of a murder, it really makes you wonder how far as a civilization we have come. There is no doubt the physical sights that are described here will draw attention, but, as I said earlier, that is really not what the story is about. I'm not sure if it is about losing innocence, growing up, or about the lack of empathy that exists in the world in which we live. Hopefully by the end of this book you can make some conclusions about some issues that are rarely discussed.

My agenda here is to tell my story as I remember it. We do not, as a society, peek under the covers on certain issues. This seems to be one topic we can at least all agree we will be participating in when our time comes.

CHAPTER 1
MY FAMILY TREE

In order to better understand how I arrived at the places and scenes we will talk about, it is important that you understand the dynamics of how I arrived at the funeral home.

My early recollections of death and the funeral business were not unlike many folks', I suppose. When my old aunt from Bayonne died, we all went to an Irish wake that seemed like it lasted an eternity. I recall much more drinking than I do mourning. When Aunt Ellen passed on, my father seemed to be the family expert on such matters—which casket would keep Aunt Ellen from being digested by insects before the week was out, the florist who did not rip folks off at a time of need, if you needed a vault to go outside the casket, who the embalmer should be, what type of mass cards were available, visiting hours, and on and on.

A funeral can be a pretty simple affair unless you know what you are doing, I guess. Understand that death is a business. It seems as if folks are very wary to go to an auto mechanic until he has proven himself, and even then you have no idea if the work done was necessary. Try applying that logic to your local funeral home. It drives folks to think about things that can be fairly unpleasant. When a funeral home advises a sobbing parent that their daughter's body will necessitate a "closed casket" due to her injuries in last night's car crash, what exactly is that criteria? Must the body be in multiple pieces? Must the head be intact? Who makes the call? The level of trust goes well beyond knowing if you transmission in your Passat has gone bad, yet we rarely will push back on that decision.

Regarding closed caskets, I can tell you that, in most instances when a funeral director makes a decision to close a casket, it typically is a result of one of two things: either the damage is not repairable or the funeral home does not have the skills to get the job done. I have witnessed my dad spend over twelve hours reconstructing a body for viewing that many folks would not have done. Why? Knowing my father, it was because it was a situation like the one described above, where closure would be next to impossible for the family to bear; they just need to see their daughter one more time.

The skills involved in getting a damaged corpse in a presentable state are truly underappreciated, if indeed you are looking to view the body. I have always admired some religions that have no interest in the physical aspect of death. They, I believe, have come to the correct conclusion. When you die, your body is no longer part of "the plan."

My dad was always somewhat amazed when folks would come in to the wake for the first time. Typically the family would come in first, and inevitably someone in the family would make the statement, "She sure looks great." This comment would often be appropriate for older folks who have suffered and withered away over time. My father would, in his mind, say, "Looks great? She's fucking dead!"

The idea of looking great and being dead is something only possible in the mind of the person who has to say it. You will not hear a funeral director, in the confessional, say, "I embalmed some old lady last night, and she looks great."

The first recollection I have of my dad working in a funeral home was around 1964. I was eight years old, and my father was an embalmer at Goldsticker, a Jewish home for funerals in Newark, New Jersey. Something that occurred to me later was that Newark, preriots, was a pretty wealthy place, and my father, who was raised Roman Catholic, was working in a Jewish funeral home. I always thought that was odd.

I do recall that, on Saturdays, my Dad would take me to work with him, but not the type of "take-your-child-to-work day" that happens in today's corporate world. I'm not really sure what his motivation was, but it seemed like a neat thing at the time. It was here I met my first official funeral director. He was a short Jewish guy who dressed well and had the largest Cadillac that was ever built.

I remember looking with amazement at the "fins" on the back of his car. It was George Jetson–like. But that car was just the start. Hearses, flower cars, and limousines that were all the size of small trucks resided in the parking lot. Whatever this guy was doing, he was getting paid well to do it. At the same time, we were not exactly living large. This became my first lesson in the world of business hierarchy.

I'm getting ahead of myself though. My dad, as far as I can tell, started working in and around the funeral business in the early 1960s. Up until that point he was a carpenter for the Standard Oil Co. in Elizabeth, New Jersey. He was a WWII veteran who flew twenty-seven B-29 bombing missions over Japan, was stationed in Guam and Tinian, and was quick to point out that he was the only serviceman on the island of Tinian who sold ice-cold beer out of his tent. The tropical climate and remote location made this business model a win.

His draw to the funeral business was by way of his father and grandfather, both of whom where funeral directors and licensed embalmers. My dad's father was a navy man who worked most of his life at homes in Elizabeth, New Jersey. My recollections of his funeral work were not memorable. One thing I did recall was that the owners of the funeral home seemed to be, again, quite wealthy. They dressed well, drove big cars, and had soft hands. The funeral home itself was gigantic. It was white and soaked in lights. Its huge columns were impressive. It seemed like a lot of fuss for the cause.

My great-grandfather's funeral story is a bit more interesting. Although I never met P. T., he apparently was a pretty tough character. The family lived in northwest Pennsylvania in a town called

DuBois. Route 80 has since put it somewhat on the map. As a young child I remember visiting this very small town. Apparently Irish immigrants went west to work in the local coal mines.

P. T. was the local sheriff and funeral director. Talk about a closed-loop operation. It is still unclear if P. T. was in the funeral business out of opportunity or because of some connection back to southern Ireland.

The family tree, by the time it got to my branch, had three generations of funeral directors. How does something like that happen? It was just my luck. The funeral business in those days was not something a youngster aspired to be in. I'm not certain, but I doubt that has changed over the years. If your six-year-old comes home from kindergarten and says he wants to be a fireman, you pat him on the head, encourage him, and move on to the next topic. If the same six-year-old comes home and states he is interested in becoming an embalmer, you worry. It is just not something folks view as a viable option. And for all the right reasons. Looking back on my own school days, I do not think I realized till much later how other kids viewed what my family did, where we lived (in a funeral home), and what it all meant. This was especially true in my grammar schools days. We literally lived in a funeral home that was around the corner from the church and school.

I can pick out a funeral home, just driving by, even if it has no signs. I guess I'm just used to what they look like. Big buildings usually, sedate yet formal, parking, shrubs, and lights. It also seems that many of the older funeral homes are near the center of town, near the church and the casket maker, I suppose.

Once you were in the apartment upstairs, it was hard to tell. As we got older, the downstairs became the sight of some great parties. We would use the smoking lounge for indoor hockey, with customers just one doorway down the hall. As kids became braver, I was able to get some to peek. Usually it was enough to just see the casket room. If I run into someone from years ago, they remember those visits. It's no surprise I have some long-term memories as well.

One highlight of parties at the home was the baby in a bottle. We had an infant who was born premature and found in a drainpipe in Rahway. Kids chasing a baseball found it, thinking it was a doll. The underdeveloped child was placed in a bottle of formaldehyde. We would take the bottle, place a candle on top, and have séances. It was pretty creepy stuff—in a funeral home, dead body in the room, candles in the dark. I never knew what happened to that baby. Another unfinished story.

There is a strong connection between death, the funeral business, and the church. I know you cannot audit the church, but I would like to know just how big a business death and funerals are in the church. It must be a big business. It has a never ending customer list. I'm not sure of all the connections between death, the funeral business, and religion, but they are all leveraging each other to make money. That is the bottom line. It is curious. Big business.

The ceremony of death and a funeral has really become a social event here in America. First you die. The circumstances surrounding the "how" often drives the overall size of your last social event. In other words, if you live to the ripe old age of ninety-six and die peacefully in your sleep (something it seems we all wish for), most of your friends have already died, and your demise was, although not admitted to, not unexpected. This will attract a loyal but small gathering, unless, of course, you did something amazing.

If, on the other hand, you are fifty-four with four kids and a wife, and you're recently retired, folks really take it hard. This all seems logical for human nature. The question is, how does the funeral "business" view these two events? Case number two may involve multiple days of wake, more limos, more flowers, more of everything. Never lose sight that it is very much a business.

I always felt for the folks whose mom and dad died. Kids my age. One day Mom's helping with school, and the next day she is gone. And they would end up downstairs. It was interesting; kids would have a funeral at our place and not really connect me living there, or maybe they did and I didn't notice. When a big family comes to a funeral, it always seems calmer. There is a sense of hope when you are surrounded by loved ones.

Kids' funerals are by far the hardest for all involved. The faces of parents who come in to either ID kids or view the body are not easily forgotten. In the days before digital technology, when someone died and his ID could not be confirmed, a relative would have to come to actually see the body. It was often very traumatic. My dad would clean the person up the best he could, but it still was what it was. Young folks seemed to be getting killed in an unusual rate during this time in cars. We had Vietnam, and just the usual flow of death.

If you are a funeral home owner, a big funeral is something that sometimes just happens for reasons not realized or known. Other times you are just lucky. At least luckier than your customer.

My father loved a big funeral. The excitement around "the home" on the day of a big funeral, of someone none of us really knew, was amazing. It was contagious. For someone's family it might have been the saddest day in their life, and for us it felt like Christmas day.

That is the odd thing about working in and around this business. It becomes your job, and the emotional part is nowhere to be found. It is not a case of being emotionally cold or of lacking empathy. My father could not fall into those categories, but I have seen him in some pretty difficult situations. If he had not been the way he was, I'm not sure how some of these customers would have managed. He was a rock in the midst of tragedy and suffering.

Another interesting aspect of this business is the confidentiality that a funeral director will have access to. If your teenage son committed suicide, if Aunt Mary hung herself in the basement, if the local priest died of liver failure due to too much church wine, you knew it. Uncle Bob did not cut his toenails. We know. Aunt Mary had a boob job. We know.

One interesting tip for men: When I was about ten years old and working down in the embalming room with my dad, he was in the process of showing me the business. He opened the top draw of a white metal cabinet. It was filled with a virtual gold mine. Cash, drugs, jewelry, guns, you name it. He explained that most men had something hidden somewhere, usually cash, anywhere between $10.00 and $100.00. Not a lot of cash, but enough back in those days.

In retrospect, the point that strikes me is that my father never seemed to take advantage of the situation. It seemed no one but he and the deceased knew that this cash was where it was. It was meant to be hidden by someone who may have said to themselves, "I'll spend this on myself before I die." Well, we will see about that. I'm also sure there is some deep-rooted issue with men that makes them hide small sums of cash like this. It seems my dad did not ever take the cash. It sat there till it got big, and then he would give it to the church, or at least to a priest.

My Dad did have one passion: belts. We had more belts than anyone on the East coast. Whenever we had guests in the embalming room, they would be offered a belt. All colors, styles, silver buckles. 42, 54, 34—you name the size. It is something that the family *never* asks to have back. If the belt industry knew this, they could really capitalize. Used belts.

Back to the family tree. I have two sisters who never really had an interest in the funeral business. In the mid '60s it was not often that women were in the business. That being said, one of my dad's best friends from embalming school was a woman. She was a very nice lady whose sister had a long ongoing affair with my dad. I did not know this at the time, but apparently this woman, who worked in the church (there it is again) around the corner, was keeping the parish a bit happier in her own way.

My sisters, Pat and Carole, did not have much of an interest in the business and moved on as young girls did back then. By the time 1968 rolled around, my dad was making his sixth request to build a funeral home in Roselle, New Jersey. The previous variance requests had all been turned down for various reasons. Mostly the reasons where related to folks not wanting to live by a funeral home. I lived *in* a funeral home not *by* one. Carole and Pat were married and moved out by the time we were finally approved.

Three silent partners backed my father's business license, personality, and street smarts and gave him the financial backing needed. I remember the partners being very controlling and busting my dad's chops about everything. He still never took that money in the draw. Anyway, in April of 1968, my dad's dream came true: his very own "Funeral Home."

He was at the building site every day. It was a beautiful new building. And it had an elevator! To be ten years old with an elevator in your house was very cool, no matter the price.

I remember enormous amounts of detail about the construction of the funeral home. I recall the special care that went into the site where the embalming room was to be located. I never, at that time, understood why the elevator stopped waist high when it reached the embalming room. Later I became aware of the fact that it stopped at that point so that the "customer" could be moved easily onto the embalming table for his or her "prep."

The room was to be a heavy tile, one that could easily be cleaned of blood and chemicals, with oversized drains all over the place. A scale hanging from the ceiling. A freezer you could walk into and lay down. It needed to go to a temperature that was below freezing. I do know it kept very cold beer. The icebox, the scale, the drains, the elevator, all ended up having very practical business applications. All that was missing were the customers. It was hard to put it all together back then.

CHAPTER 2
LIFE AT THE HOME

I do not remember the exact day we moved into the funeral home in Roselle, New Jersey... We paid extra to get an easy-to-remember phone number. Apparently there was a belief that when someone is in a state of grief, they can recall a seven-digit number. It seemed to me no matter how easy the number was, folks would not remember the number to the funeral home they were going to call. This was not the pizza business. But we tried everything to drum up business.

The apartment upstairs was really quite nice. I had my own good-sized bedroom for the first time I could remember. Wall-to-wall carpeting. This may have been a first in the entire clan. There was another apartment in the rear that we rented over the years to some interesting and not-so-interesting folks. You get a versatile mix of folks who are willing to rent an apartment above a funeral home. We had all sorts.

The real story was downstairs. The newest funeral home in Union County was worthy of my dad's dreams. Huge white columns out front. His name in lights. Two large viewing rooms that could be divided into four if necessary. His own office. Downstairs was a "smoking lounge." That was a big deal back in the '70s. Apparently folks that went to funerals smoked when they got there. They never made the connection till later. This room was also used for some of the more wild misadventures of my youth.

Also in the basement was the "showroom." This was where the next of kin would pick out the casket they wanted to put their lost relative in for the final drop. The circumstances in this room can swing wildly. I have been in there with folks joking about how their ninety-year-old mom loved cherry wood. I have also been there when it must have been dreamlike for some soul in a very difficult situation—any sudden death, a child's death. The room was always the same room, but it could take on a different feeling depending on the situation. It seemed like the lighting would change for certain circumstances, like someone knew to tone it up or down a bit.

Lights are a big part of being dead. I recall much thought going into the lighting in the viewing rooms. Think makeup. The last room that was downstairs was the above-mentioned embalming room—surely the center of action, other than the cash register, in the funeral business.

Although I do not recall the date we moved into the funeral home, I do remember our grand opening. It was a big event in town. The mayor came out, ribbons were cut, beer was drunk. No one died, so it was a day with mixed emotions. You have a very interesting dynamic if you work in the funeral business. It is really pretty simple business. If someone dies, you make money. My dad would never wish bad luck or hardship on anyone; he was not wired that way. With all that being said, however, it is a business.

Make no mistake. Physically living in a funeral home did not have an immediate impact either way on my daily life. We did have a big parking lot, which resulted in a basketball court and a good stickball yard. The kids in the neighborhood were very nice. This had been about the fifth house in Roselle I had lived in the last seven years. I knew everyone in town, but we never stood still. It was hard to get settled down. I'm not surprised that now, later in life, I have become very reluctant to move. I'll settle for less instead of moving.

Anyway, we were living in a funeral home. If there is one thing you need in a funeral home to succeed, it is customers.

Funeral homes without dead people are nice buildings that, if you did not know the background, could be rented out for a wedding. So, we waited. Some folks knew my dad and came in and made prearrangements.

This is very common now. Back then I think they were just trying to help my dad. More than a few ninety-year-old grandparents were on our preapproved list. No money down. We just needed activity. They were customers in waiting. Today it seems the financial institutions and the government have both gotten into the prepay funeral business. My father was not making any money. He was just trying to "get the first one."

It seems dying and the funeral business can be a bit like baseball, at least for a new funeral home. Have you ever heard the baseball adage, "Once we get our first hit…we will get something going…we'll score some more"? It's the same thing in the funeral business. Get that first one, and you're on the road to success. We waited, and waited, and waited. None of the good people were dying. All Protestants, Blacks, Hispanics, non-Irish. We didn't lose any. We just had a poor pool of candidates. Our luck seemed to be running out.

Dad was attending every Moose, Elk, Hibernian, K of C, Mason, and AMA meeting he could get to. If you were near death in Union County in 1968, my dad shook your hand. It is a tough business to self-generate.

Then, in the most parochial of terms, our luck broke. Our first customer, age eighty-eight. He was presigned eight months earlier at the request of his doctor, who said he would be gone by the weekend…eight months ago. Keep that in mind about doctors as well. Well, this was a nice kick-off. Bronze casket, one-day visiting, very high-margin vault—all on a presign. Dad was encouraged to say the least.

After that I lost count. We started having funerals three to four times a week. Mostly everyone who died and belonged to St. Joseph's Church went to our home. The success of the home seemed to be a bit of a surprise to everyone. If my dad had a background in business, I'm sure it would have been a much more profitable entity. But he did not.

I think many folks in the funeral business realized there was a lot of cash around the business in those days. I'm sure some folks were playing the game better than we were. Talking about money when someone died was taboo back then—"When I get the insurance check, I'll pay you"—although my dad did have a great idea to drive business. That was also legal.

In New Jersey in 1970, the county morgue was not as it is today, centralized, etc. It was bid out to a local funeral home, whose job it was to pick up the body of any homicide, suicide, sudden/accidental death, or a death for which no doctor would sign a death certificate. We had expanded our marketing and sales channel overnight. This would be the biggest thing to ever happen to *the* home, my father, and this story. It gave him what he wanted: exposure. It gave me what I did not want, although at the time I did not know: exposure.

After we became the county morgue, life around the home changed. It became very busy. My dad's name was in the local newspaper every day. It was not uncommon to see him on the front page, either in a picture removing some sorry mess from the scene of the crime or the name of our home as the new place of residence for the new customer. Good thing we had a cooler.

This was all happening as I was graduating from the local grammar school and moving on to high school. My schoolmates really did not pay too much attention to the funeral home and what was going on inside. I'm not sure if they did not think about it or if they were afraid.

My best friend from the young days was Kevin. He lived around the corner from one of the sites where my dad wanted to build. We had known each other since the first grade, and although at times we went in difference directions, we always came back to one another.

Kevin was one year ahead of me at school and was an early, true, bass-playing, long-haired hippie. He had red hair, was tall, and always stood up for me in our town, which was a pretty tough place back then. I recall like yesterday lying on the floor of his den, a tile floor, and playing with the new invention of the day, "Hot Wheels." As the cars sped, we would try to create wrecks and spinouts. It all seemed so innocent and simple. I would never dream of how those thoughts would come back in colors so real. It still seems impossible to believe after all these years.

Kevin's family was pretty religious. He had a sister who was a few years older than us. He also had an older brother who was rarely seen in person. It reminded me of Richie Cunningham's brother, Chuck, from *Happy Days*. Anyway, Kevin and I were best friends, and it was a great time to be our age. We were having a great time.

It was the late '60s. Although hippies were emerging, hoods still ran in the streets. We were somewhere between Buddy Holley and John Lennon. Our days consisted of getting home from school and going out to play. Unlike in today's world, I remember no sense of the fear that seems to exist today. Letting your eight-year-old child leave on his bike for the day was not considered unusual.

At this time my dad was trying to get a zoning approval for his dream business. Before this it was really not all that evident to me that we were working in the funeral business. He would leave in the morning in a suit and come home. But the hours were not the same all the time. I did not give it much thought.

Dad attempted to get the zoning and was rejected on five different occasions. He had two things against him. The first was that the business he was trying to open was not really desirable to the neighbors. I never did understand that, but I was close to it from a very young age. The second was political clout and money. He was too honest early on to suspect the real world worked like that. And even if he wanted, he did not have the funds.

There were many disappointments in the process. We would move from location to location what seemed like every year to chase the approval. We lived in some tiny apartments and some really cool old houses that were planned for renovation.

The houses my dad picked for possible renovation were all old beautiful homes built in the late 1800s. The Higgins estate would have made a perfect funeral home. The building was really something. We also attempted to get a house zoned that included, as one of its early renters, Thomas Edison. All the houses were old and looked like they could be where Gomez Adams hangs his hat. As we moved from location to location trying to get the necessary approval, my exposure to death was yet to accelerate. In the end, we built a new building anyway.

As this was going on, Kevin and I continued to play army and ride our bikes. Vietnam was at the top of the news but not at the top of our minds. We were still too young. The war did provide a small blip to business. A really neat older kid from my neighborhood was killed in Vietnam. I remember him being like Tarzan when we played in the backyard. His house had really tall trees that Leslie could climb like a monkey. They said he was killed in action, and I do not doubt that one bit.

We did not handle his funeral, but I visited the Vietnam Memorial Wall and scratched his name on a piece of paper. War deaths all get the same casket—silver, sturdy, government-issue. No markup for the funeral home either. It really hit me that he was there one day and gone the next. It would turn out I would see more of that than I would have liked to.

The importance of this time in my story is the relationship that Kevin and I had. We were best buddies. It may just be a small boy thing, but when you have a feeling of comfort about someone who likes you for who you are, it feels good! Kevin is one of the main reasons I wrote this book. Our relationship, his fate, the funeral business—all linked at once.

When I was in high school, our family treated death for what it was—the business by which we put food on the table, heated our house, drove cars, and went on vacation. Death was in our best interest. What a paradox. Nobody in their right mind would be rooting for death. I think our view was, if you have to die, you should, at minimum, let my clan prosper from your bad luck.

I mentioned that Kevin's fate was an unforgettable moment in my life as it related to the funeral business and death, a moment that would put me in a helpless and unmanageable situation for the next thirty-plus years.

Back in those days Kevin, myself, and many of our classmates would go camping. Camping, as we called it back then, consisted of two main things: pot and beer. I remember once having a bag of cookies. The real purpose of these trips was to get a good buzz on with friends. Tunes, campfires, and lots of laughs.

One weekend in February 1980, I was camping in Sussex County in northwest New Jersey, a really beautiful part of the state of New Jersey. Back then it was far less developed. It was one of the usual trips. We stayed the whole weekend, and I really have no recollection of anything that happened that was special. Same friends, same routine.

This was pre–cell phones so it was not like we were texting our parents as I do with my teens today. The weekend concluded as planned. I drove home on Sunday afternoon, hurting from three days of whooping it up and not sleeping. Home, as a reminder, was "the home." I parked my car and directed my smelly, hung-over self to the side door of the home. Both apartments above the funeral home had their own entrances. It was at that moment that something unusual happened.

My mom opened the door and was standing there. She must have heard my VW Bug pull in. She had a look on her face that was not anger, as I expected, but one of sorrow. My mom was not a very emotional Irish lass. Growing up one of twelve in Depression-era Jersey City does not really soften you up. The look in my mother's eyes made me think something bad had happened. These moments seem like they last forever, but they were really only a few seconds.

She asked if I had spoken to anyone or seen anyone since I had returned from camping. I said I had not. I forget the exact words, but she said there had been a terrible car crash in Kenilworth the night before. She said three boys had died in the crash. Then, as if it were in slow motion, she said the following: "Kevin was one of the boys killed. Your father is downstairs with the boys right now."

My mom followed me up the stairs. My hangover was gone. When you first hear something like that, I suppose there is really not a good or bad way to tell someone. My mom did the best she could.

The thought that Kevin and Craig and Wayne, friends of mine, were downstairs made me sick. I knew too much about this. Kevin was too close. I did not need to go downstairs and see it, although later I would. I had seen this many times before, just never this close.

When I speak of the perspective of death that not many have, this is a great example. It is tough enough to grieve, but if you have the visual reality in your mind, you really "get the picture."

I do not recall the next few days. I do recall going to Kevin's wake. It was very crowded, and for some reason I did not want to be seen. I went at the busiest time, paid my respects to Kevin, signed the book, grabbed a prayer card, and walked out the door. That night I made a decision that I would never work in the funeral business again. A promise that, to the dismay of my family, I kept.

It took me a while to come to grips with the decision. I could not believe I was standing at the side of an embalming table, guts up to my elbows, and wondering if I was making the right call. I knew the business was my dad's pride. But by the time Kevin was killed, the job had become less interesting. Now I only wanted to go out on pickups that were "interesting." Then, after I processed what had happened, I knew I wanted to be as far away from dead bodies as I could. I may not have been able to undo what had been done, but I could stop it from continuing.

I still carry Kevin's mass card. I remember Kevin's wake as if it were the past one. I cannot believe that some folks' lives are taken at such a young age. They sure miss a lot.

CHAPTER 3
EARLY MEMORIES

It's funny now, but it never gave me pause that I lived in a funeral home. I just cannot figure it out why it was so normal, but it really felt separate, like it was not really part of me. It was my dad's job. The added fortune of being then connected to the medical examiner's office was a set of circumstances that resulted in my being in on some of the big-time autopsies of the '70s and '80s, some claim to fame that not many kids on the block could match. Now that I think of witnessing someone's head being taken apart, guts all over the room. I would leave, go upstairs, eat a pizza from Naples Pizzeria, and watch Batman.—going from exposed bowels to a small pizza with extra cheese and sausage. Not bad for a kid.

Being a ten-year-old child living and working in a funeral home did have a certain aspect of notoriety—access to places, crossing the police yellow tape in a very casual manner. A fact: a dead body cannot be removed from where it lies until the medical examiner arrives on the scene. It should not even be moved. This created a somewhat important role for my dad and myself. Many police officers, detectives, and EMS workers would ask what I was doing at the scene of a particular crash behind the yellow tape. When I told them who I was, I could walk right on by. "He's with the medical examiner."

I mentioned news coverage. It is interesting, and I would not have noticed it unless I was looking for it, but the fact is, your daily local newspaper is full of folks in various articles who are directly related to death. If you add the official notices, the obituaries, that means a significant portion of what we read is related to death, murder, car crashes, etc. Conversely, there is very little attention given to births. They even use small print for births while deaths are front-page news.

My dad's idea was that having the county morgue was really not for the money; you were paid a nominal amount to pick up the bodies. The real win was in the free advertising. The name of our home was in every article written about every murder, plane crash, car crash, suicide, overdose, hit by a car, hit by a train, and parachute jump. They all ended with "…and the body was removed to our county morgue in Roselle." It was marketing genius. We paid nothing and had our names on the front page more often than the local politicians.

I started working for my dad when I was about nine years old. The first duty was pretty minor stuff: bringing in the flowers, cleaning the lounge, and running to the courthouse for death certificates. All pretty innocent stuff compared to what was going to come. There was real money to be had, but you needed to get closer to the customer, if you know what I mean.

In those days my father had a Plymouth station wagon that we used to pick up bodies. It was black and even had a portable red light we could use when we needed to get through traffic. I always found it interesting that we had a red light on the roof, as if the customer we were going to meet had few options if we were to get stuck in traffic. I think it just made my dad feel he had unlimited access to any crime scene.

Anyway, I began joining my dad when I was about ten whenever he would go to pick up dead people. First, the simple stuff: hospitals. In case you hadn't noticed, hospitals have a very large entryway with valet parking, flower shops, information desks. If the hospital is not able to save you, the morgue exist is a bit less fancy. Typically located by the garbage disposal area for some odd reason, the door to the morgue is not usually marked and is always locked.

Hospital pickups were the easiest: slide the poor soul off the table onto the stretcher, and off you go. Back then I was paid $20 cash for each pickup. I remember the first time I got $20 for what seemed like very little work. I was thrilled.

One of my earliest confrontations with a pickup of a violent death was in Linden off St. Georges Avenue. We were called to remove a twenty-eight-year-old male who died as a result of "cleaning his gun." Dad and I had our usual "sorry-about-this" look on our faces. A few cops were mulling around outside, smoking butts and laughing. That meant no family was around. Always better.

There was a narrow walkway that wound up to the porch where the man had been cleaning his gun. It seemed he had not only cleaned the gun but cleaned his head clear off his body. He was sitting on the edge of a couch. The cleaning fluid was on the table in front of him. He had positioned the high-powered rifle so that it was aimed at himself, had been cleaning, and *POW*! At close range it literally blew his head off his neck. Shattered it in millions of small chunks of red slush. His torso was resting back in the chair, hands relaxed at his side. All very comfortable, except for the missing head.

I was walking into the place where the gentleman had had the unfortunate run-in with the gun. I stepped in something on the way into the house. I was not really sure what it was. When I checked the bottom of my foot, I discovered a piece of brain stuck to my shoe. As I focused on the area around me, I noticed that there were many pieces of fresh brain in the grass where I was standing. When the gun went off, the man was on his screened-in back porch. The high-powered rifle had removed his head from his torso and shattered it into a million pieces, one of which was stuck to my new Chuck Taylors. Now I was starting to earn my $20.

Another well-earned twenty happened right in front of the funeral home in Roselle. Two local guys were leaving the Dutch Room Tavern, a seedy little joint that drew a seedy crowd— bikers, drunks, and people hiding from other people.

The two guys walked across the street and got into their car. One guy determined that he should have taken a piss before he left, and he headed back to the bar to do so. He got out and started walking. At that moment, three kids in a car came up Second Avenue, traveling an estimated 110 mph. Needless to say, my advice to everyone is pee next to the car. This guy wishes he did.

But that is not the really interesting part for the morgue keeper. When we arrived at the scene there were lots of cops and the road was blocked off A body could be seen up a ways, underneath a parked car. It appeared his final resting place was about one hundred feet up the road. My father and I began to trek up the road to recover our reason for being there and for me to get my $20. We reviewed the situation, and my dad said he would pull the victim out from under the car and that I should hold the stretcher in place. As he pulled, the body actually came out much easier than expected—for good reason: The guy had been cut perfectly in half at the belt. This was one leather belt my father was not going to add to his collection. We did have a slight problem though. Where was the rest of him?

Word spread quickly of the missing half, and the hunt was on. About two blocks down the road, under another parked car, lay the bottom half of my customer. All was well again. I tried to hit my dad up for a double fee to no avail. Just as an aside, we received a call the next day that a resident had found a strange item under this car and called police. It was our customer's liver. I had to go out again. Three separate pickups for one body. Surely one could argue my dad got the best of his resources that day. People find their demise in very strange ways. It always seems to come out of nowhere.

I mentioned earlier that my dad would work forever on putting folks back together. This guy's funeral was at our funeral home. My dad put the guy back together, minus his liver, and his family never knew the better. It was an open casket. Everyone mourned, and no one cared that I got screwed on my pickup fee.

The embalming room was a sight to behold. Lots of neat gadgets. A saw that could cut through your skull without harming the soft tissue. A scale to weigh organs on—that I used to weigh quarter pounds of weed. The freezer was quite an item itself. It could fit a family of four comfortably. Stacked we could get up to eight, but thankfully never needed to go to that capacity. Every picnic in the area asked to keep their kegs at our house, another cross-sell opportunity we could have taken advantage of, especially during the holidays. Lots of small surgical blades, clamps, scissors, etc., all used at various stages of autopsies and embalmings.

The embalming machine was also another highlight. My father shopped for it like it was a new car. We went to several vendors, all of whom competed for the right to pump the blood from our customers. The sound that machine made was something you would never forget, the steady beat of blood being pumped out and embalming fluid being pumped in. It had a ringing tang like a toy of some sort. It was annoying and yet nondistracting. It kept the pace. *Tick*—blood out—*tock*—fluid in. The whole process takes about three hours. It always seemed odd that the blood was pumped down the drain and into the standard sewer.

Embalming is an art more than a science, although my dad's knowledge of the human body was quite extensive. He was familiar by sight with every organ and non-organ type material I would see. It became very commonplace to be helping out in the embalming room.

Embalming fluid is something that warrants mentioning. Strong, really strong stuff. Formaldehyde. It was very expensive and was handled with care. It could really burn you bad if misused. Just around the time I became aware of such things, folks were trying to get a hold of embalming fluid. They would dunk cigarettes in it and smoke them. It was supposed to be quite a rush. Clearly this had to be pretty dangerous. Older kids had approached me, but I insisted it was under lock and key and that I had no access to it. That was not exactly the truth. It was still one thing I did not try. I knew what that stuff did, and it was crazy.

It does make you consider the whole proposition. Why would we fill our dead relatives with poison to preserve them, decorate them with makeup, dress them up, and then bury them? It really makes no sense at all.

If you ask folks who work around the business what the worst physical aspect of the job is, they would say the smell. There is nothing worse than the smell of flesh that has been rotting on a warm summer's day. It is incredible.

This is one area where even my dad had met his match. My dad once picked up a body in an apartment in Newark many years ago. It was a hot summer day. Always is. He pulled up in front of an apartment building to find the police standing around with gas masks in their hands, many of them getting sick on the ground. This was not a good sign. If I had been there, this would not have been a $20 billing.

My dad asked what was up, and the sergeant explained they had had calls regarding a smell up on one of the higher floors. After searching, the police had narrowed it down to an upper apartment, a one-bedroom fixer-upper with a view. At least there used to be a view. A closer look at the windows and you could tell they had been painted black. My dad headed up the stairs, re-fusing a gas mask but wisely removing his false teeth. The stench was incredible as he entered the apartment. It turns out the win-dows had not been painted; they were covered with flies, so thick you could not see the light of day out the window. Flies love rotten meat.

My dad walked into the bedroom where the body was and saw something he had never seen before. The body was not at all visible, but, instead, lying on the ground was a two-hundred-pound mass of moving maggots. It was the most incredible sight. Lunch was being served. Somehow that day he got the body back to the freezer and had it set as cold as it would go. That does not kill maggots, but it slows them down. To kill them you need to get a gasoline-type product and douse them. Nasty stuff.

My dad said that about two weeks after that he farted and it smelled like that body. It had permeated his skin. It took weeks to finally rid himself of the smell. My father shared this experience with me at a young age. The price for picking up a "floater," as they were called in the business, starts at $100. Of course, this was an extreme case. Most folks have people around so that, if they should die, someone is there there to find them in a fair amount of time—or, at least, before the windows are blacked out.

While attending college, I served my apprenticeship toward getting my embalming license. In order to enter the McAllister's

Embalming School in Manhattan, you had to serve a kind of residency for funeral directors. It consisted of assisting on ninety embalmings and body preps over a two-year period. Of course, having dad to help made it easier, but it's still a strange out-of-school activity for 1975. I labored through the process and did what I needed to. It had to have appeared that I was not enjoying it, and I wondered if my dad picked up on this. He was looking at the fourth generation in the business as I was trying to satisfy him and get out.

CHAPTER 4

IT COST TO BE DEAD

The idea of the Catholic funeral process is really amazing. I would guess that, outside of a few other items they dominated, such as weddings and baptisms, death is a top five moneymaker for the Catholic Church. The pomp and circumstance around dying that the funeral industry has developed, partnering with guilt-ridden Catholics, is truly bazaar.

The entire industry is built around guilt that some close family member will be languishing in purgatory unless you provide, on average, about $12,000 for a proper burial. I really do not think that dead people have any inkling or desire to be stuffed with chemicals, have makeup painted on them, and have their family spend $400 to drive in a limousine to an empty field with cement scattered about. It really defies logic, but that is exactly the point.

When survivors are in mental state where they are vulnerable, a good funeral director can empty their wallets quicker than a roulette wheel can. The funeral business becomes like the car rental business, except you are not in the defensive mode when you visit. Upgrades are key. A better casket, vault, tombstone. It goes on and on. "We do have this basic model, although it has been known to leak water over time…" All you can imagine is Mom floating with the worms six feet under the ground. "For a few more dollars, you can put your mind at ease…" You can see how it works.

One of the truly amazing aspects of the business is how folks are dressed in the casket. Fact one: Everyone wants to look their best for their funeral. Fact two: Dead people are hard to dress. Not very cooperative. This creates an interesting situation for the funeral director, as well as another financial opportunity. Folks typically go out to buy a suit or dress for the deceased. I have seen some pretty high-end stuff be dropped off so we could get Pop looking his Sunday best to rot in for eternity.

As I said, getting a dead person to put on a suit is not as easy as it sounds, although the industry has made it quite easy. It actually was very simple. We would cut the suit or dress up the back and basically pin it to our customers. I have seen $2,000 suits, brand-new off the rack, ripped up the back. No one would know the better, but my advice to you, if you insist on dressing someone up for the farewell, is to not spend too much.

The idea for the naming of the book comes from this still challenging part of the funeral business. You have these new clothes, a big guest list, people fussy about looks, under the lights. It's lots of pressure. The story goes that the older funeral directors, set with the task of moving uncooperative customers from table to table, getting them dressed, etc., came up with the perfect solution. They determined that if they could simply switch heads to a fixed set of bodies that were already dressed, they could save hours.

It started in the military where everyone had the same uniforms. Simply switching heads became a practice wherever this highly efficient model could be implemented. From the perspective of everyone, it is a win-win. Do you really care if those were not your uncle's feet? As long as you see his face and smile, you're covered.

I have shared many different versions of when switching heads became the only practical thing the undertaker could do. Folks stand in disbelief. If you believe the fact that folks always try to shortcut everything, save a buck or a minute, this can keep you up at night. So, keep in mind that if Grandma has her usual smile, but has a tattoo on her ass, all may not be what it appears to be!

Jewelry is another accessory I should weigh in on. Wedding bands, broaches, pins, service metals, etc. Do not assume that what you left in the casket is what is being lowered into the ground. My dad was an honest sort when it came to this type of thievery, but it was common in the business at the time. There are certain folks—gypsies come to mind—who actually put cash in the casket. Trust me on this. You are not the last one to see what is actually in a casket when it is closed. I left my mom a bottle of Dewar's and was there for the closing, so I'm sure she still has it, but the same cannot be said for most caskets that go down. If Mom had a great piece of jewelry, let her wear it, and then remove it prior to burial and give it to a living relative.

I have noticed lately when going to funerals that folks are dressing their dead relatives, as well as themselves, less formally than in the old days. I went to a friend's funeral last year, and his wife had him dressed in his Washington Redskins jersey, jeans, and sneakers. Die like you live...I like it. Just keep in mind that even that Redskins jersey was ripped up the back and pinned onto him. It is the only way to do it. I'm just not sure if I am ready to make a commitment to a football team that is in place for eternity...or until the bugs gobble me up.

Another side business that flows from funerals is flowers. It is not as big as it used to be, but many folks' first instinct when they hear of a death is to send flowers. It is a nice sentiment but really a somewhat wasteful spending of hard-earned cash. Once the funeral home location is announced, either through the newspaper or word of mouth, folks begin calling the local florist. These folks, being opportunistic types, have developed an entire "line" of flowers so that you can personalize your message. Bleeding hearts, rosary beads, custom designs, baskets, sprays, and on and on. It is no mistake that the Church again shows up, influencing what we buy and send off.

There is no doubt that when you walk into the visiting room at a funeral home, the vision and smell of the flowers can be soothing. But keep in mind this is a two-day affair. Not many folks would spend $150 on flowers with the understanding that they had to throw them away in two days, even if there was not a wilting flower among them. But that is just the business case in this scenario. This allows florists to dump all the older inventory on these poor souls who feel they are doing the right thing. They also use the cheapest, non-sell products they have. It makes good business sense. I cannot tell you how many thousands of dollars used to go to waste the day of the funeral.

One thing I will tell you is that if you ever have the chance to visit a funeral director's home—his real home—you will notice a wonderful array of flowers. After viewing this for several years, my dad had a great idea. Every Saturday morning I would deliver to all of the nursing homes in the area our extra surplus of flowers. I think Dad's intention was good, but to me it just gave the old folks a sneak preview of what was to come. Stiff as a board, filled with chemicals, mouth sewn shut, eye caps in place, ripped clothes, and stale flowers. What a great send-off.

Another angle on flower was the rental of a flower car, provided, of course, to those families who had so many friends and family that they sent more flowers than could fit into the hearse. This was a home run. An extra $300 for a special car to drive your flowers to the garbage dump after they leave the cemetery. Take my advice on this one: If you feel compelled to spend money to honor a fallen friend, send it somewhere that it can be of some use. The American Cancer Society, autism research, even the Boy Scouts. But do not waste your money on flowers. I'm sure I will be hearing from the Society for the Expansion of the Flower Industry, but I could care less. That is why we have lawyers.

Another good one that is linked directly to the church is mass cards. The concept is simple. You can reserve a mass to be said in honor of your lost soul. What that entails is a priest mentioning the name of the deceased at the mass: "This mass honors the demise of…"

A few things on this. Number one: The church, in its heart of hearts, has determined that this mentioning of someone who has been dropping funds in the basket every week should have a fee attached to it, usually no less than $25. Take a few minutes and see how long it takes to say your name. Divide that by $25 and multiply it by how many times it can be said in an hour. That's 3600 times per hour at $25 a hit, or $90,000 per hour. That's more than Alex Rodriguez makes in a good hour. In fact, the entire Yankee team does not make that in an hour. It's all about how you position it.

I believe these mass cards should come with a guarantee. Either you get into heaven, you get abbreviated time in purgatory, or you get an air conditioner in hell.

Another thing that is bothersome about this is the timing. Since many more people are dying than there are masses said, there is a backlog, often a very long backlog. It is not unusual for the mass you have dedicated to be said many years from the actual time of death. It may be me, but death is something that requires instant gratification. I want the mass the day, or, at minimum, the week of the funeral. At $90,000 per hour, you would think the Church would figure this out.

Once again, give the money to someone who can use it, or to a good research project. We live our lives usually with some sort of interest. What better way to honor someone than to have some impact on something they were interested in. Of course, if they owned a florist or were priests, the above option may not be applicable. Keep in mind, as well, that the funeral director can be involved in both of these scams. If you are from out of town and want to send flowers or get a mass card, chances are you will call the funeral director for the name of a florist or the name of the local church for the mass card. Bingo referral income. It's all about the money.

This use of the word "bingo" was purely by chance and was not intended to bring up the entertainment division of the Church's revenue-producing business model. If it seems I am picking on the Catholic Church a little, it is true. Although my dad did work in a Jewish funeral home for many years, it was the Catholic experience that really caused me to stop and think. Taking advantage of grieving folks is something they do in such a subversive way; it seems almost criminal. Catholic churches recommend Catholic funeral homes, and that is where the billings begin.

From the start, embalming preserves the body so the viewing can go on for days. This practice has slowed down a bit, but not merely what it should be. They utilize the guilt that has been engrained at an early age to ensure that you think twice about every decision. If our soul is truly on an express train to either heaven or hell, what is the point of carrying on this ritual unless there is something else involved? My guess is that that something else is money, the backbone of the Catholic Church in America. I'm not suggesting that priests are outright on the take in the business. I try not to be that cynical. But if it were really our best interest they had in mind, they might wish to take a look at the involvement they have in the entire affair.

Another offshoot of the funeral business is the cemetery business. If you really want to cause havoc in the U.S., going after the World Trade Center is a flawed plan. Attacking the Grave Diggers Union would cause much more chaos. This is especially true in warmer climate states. If you ever notice when the grave diggers go out on strike, it gets resolved fairly quickly, and for good reason.

Take the state of New Jersey, where I reside. With one week down, no grave digging causes a backlog of over 1,055 dead, rotting bodies. One week! Remember my story of the guy with the maggots. Times it by 1,055, and stand back. Not only would closure not be reached for all these families; bagpipers would be out of business, hearse drivers would be standing idle, and they would keep piling up. I'm not sure who runs the union, but I suspect it is the best salary and benefit package in the backhoe business.

If you are ever at a funeral, you will always see these guys off in the background, sitting on their yellow machines, waiting for you to hit the buffet table at the post funeral gala. Before you turn the corner, the show begins. I'm not sure if it is still the case, but these folks were not beyond having one last peek at your loved one before the dirt started to move. I suppose they would not want you to leave anything of any importance in the casket before you leave. My guess is that any valuables they find are immediately turned over to the family. I would like to understand how often that happens every year.

I mentioned the post funeral gala. This is truly the send-off we all deserve. Restaurants now specialize in these events. Talk about getting one last squeeze out of life. And, of course, the priest is always able to carve time out of his busy schedule for a free meal, a few cold beverages, and a check made out to the church for services rendered. We had more than a few honorable employees of the Church advise us that cash was also acceptable. I thought they did not pay taxes as it was. Anyway, the bottom line here is to be careful. Bring someone with you who is not as emotionally involved in the matter as yourself, and ask a lot of questions. You still will get ripped off, but you can minimize the damage.

CHAPTER 5
THE DIRTY WORK

My reasons for writing this book were not to attack the Catholic Church, the funeral industry, grave diggers, or even the florist industry. One side of me wanted people to know that, when you die, there is a very real business model in place. As with most business plans, they open their doors to make money.

The second reason I put down into words what I had felt and seen was to help myself. It is clear to me now that I am older that I should not have been exposed to many of the visions I saw at a young age. Although folks like EMS workers, firemen, and soldiers see the dark side of death and dying, not many children get a close-up view such as I did.

I am confident my father did not expose me to this with the thought of the long-term damage it may do to me. It was, for him, simply the business he had been in and owned. It made sense that he would teach his son the traits of this business, just as any carpenter or plumber would do. The fact that my siblings were girls who had no interest in the business made me the main candidate to take over. Any father who owns a business and is self-employed would want the same for his son. The fact that the business was profitable and stable also contributed to the fact that he not only did not see harm in doing this but also thought he had paved the way for me to have a successful business career in a line of work that is traditionally passed down from father to son over many generations.

Funeral directors are a very small tight-knit community. Although competitive, they are aware that there are not many of themselves, and they use that to their advantage. Their shared unique experiences create a bond. At a different time, my dad worked for many of the funeral directors in the Union and Essex County area of New Jersey. He made a fair living as an embalmer. The hours were very unpredictable, and the work was not much fun. It seemed there was quite a bit of drinking that went with the job. I was never sure, when I was younger, if it was the long hours being in the embalming room or the depressing subject matter, but I do know that our cooler always had beer in it, and it moved quickly.

Dad had one of the early beepers when they first came out. This was in case he was out picking up one dead person and another one died. Double headers. The beeper was more commonly used by my dad to get out of social events, especially family events. He would set the beeper off, tell everyone someone had died, and leave. No one could ever question him. Someone had died right in the middle of our party. No one would lie about that. Every time my mom's family came over, the beeper would go off and someone had died. He would apologize and be on his way. Most people do not question death if you use it as an excuse. It can be used to get out of work or school. My dad had a great excuse and was never questioned.

There are really two sides to the business. The behind-the-scenes part, which was not very pleasant or motivating, and the people-facing part, which required a special personality. My dad was considered an excellent embalmer, but, more importantly, he was great with people.

Death creates many different circumstances and emotions for those left behind. The circumstances of the death often were the driving force in how things played out. There is an old saying that a parent should never have to bury a child. This is very true. I have witnessed situations where parents need to take care of a child when they die. It has to be the most wrenching experience any adult can have.

Many times these situations involve kids being kids that end up bad. Two scenarios at the top of my mind are automobile accidents and drug overdoses. With drug use, the parent may or may not have a hint that their teenager is using something that may kill them. They never believe it will happen to them. The invincibility of youth convinces a kid that they can get away with anything. As we all know, this is not the case. Drug overdoses are no longer a monopoly for poor, low-class people. Everyone is in the game. And everyone is dying. I'm not in a position to preach about the drug problems we have in America, but I can tell you that it is out of control, and if we all could spend some time seeing and hearing the parents of these children, we may have a new perspective on the impact it has on the entire family.

In theory, the person who overdoses is free of the pain they were in. What they leave behind is a mess. Parents who will never recover, needing years of therapy and medication to just get through a day. Drug and alcohol abuse contribute much pain to society today, and we need to be more diligent about it. It is not a good way to die—if there is ever a good way to die—especially for a young teenager who has their life ahead of them.

The other situation that is alarming and very sad is auto accidents. This one seems more sudden and is certainly more violent. A child you have raised since birth. You watch every move they make in hopes you can prevent harm to them. From early on, their physical well-being is a focus for most parents. Then, one night, a call comes from a police officer that is every parent's nightmare. It must fell dreamlike. This cannot be happening. But it is.

Car accidents have created some of the more horrible scenes I have ever witnessed. A two-thousand-pound automobile traveling at a high rate of speed can cause more damage to the human body than you would care to think about. I have seen wrecks where the body is not badly damaged, but, for the most part, it is a bloody, mangled mess. Decapitation, limbs severed, bodies crushed to nothing is more how these situations play out.

To imagine what it was like in the moments leading up to these situations can keep you up at night. Typically kids are not alone in cars; they are out having fun. Perhaps some beers and a joint to live up to teen expectations. And then, in a moment, it is all over. The car comes to a rest, and there is silence.

I often noticed the smell at these wrecks. Oil, gasoline, and antifreeze are in the air. Some cars are unrecognizable. They say some cars are safer than others. Airbags, seatbelts, SUVs. It is all bullshit. The right amount of speed hitting a nonmoving object like a tree, and these things do nothing. I have witnessed seatbelts that have snapped from impact, as well as seatbelts that have killed people from the impact being so great. Literally cutting into their body.

We all know that mixing together the two above maladies is a recipe for something bad. Driving while on drugs or drinking is a common known killer, but until you see the damage upfront and then see the families afterwards, the puzzle is not complete.

My father never seemed to get emotionally involved in these situations. I never saw him shed a tear for these folks. It was always business as usual. Somehow I think that helped these folks. He would stay on point. Get the situation under control, and at that point in time, when everything was out of control for them, here was someone who was trying to keep the process moving with respect. He was never rude, but always firm. There were things that needed to get done, paperwork that needed to be processed, decisions that needed to be made, all at a time when the last thing these folks wanted to do was do what he was asking. I'm not sure what he felt like inside, but I did know it was one of the issues that made me turn my back on the business.

When my dad was working at other funeral homes, I visited them from time to time, like a dismal version of "take-your-kid-to-work day." It never seemed to bother me too much, and I never really go that close to the action. I do not recall seeing anything that frightened me like later scenes would. We would visit when my dad went to work on Saturdays, and I would basically hang around until he was done with whatever it was he had to do. What he was actually doing never impacted me or my friends. They never really said much about it, and I never discussed it.

When we built our own funeral home, things changed very quickly. Now we lived in the funeral home, so it was much harder to hide the fact that we were in the business. Early on the kids in the neighborhood would ask questions, but I think I was still too young to figure out just what was going on.

I do recall in the first year I was exposed to things I had never seen before or even dreamt about, but it still did not have the expected effect. You become somewhat immune to what is going on around you. I was helping Dad in work as far as I was concerned, and the money was not bad. For a twelve-year-old in 1968, $20 was a fair amount of cash to be getting. My sisters were both married and moved out by the time we moved into our home, so the family fortune had my name written all over it.

Dad talked about how he would have to change the name to Sullivan and Son Funeral Home once I made the commitment. It almost seemed like the decision of what I would do for the rest of my life had been made. It was a good healthy business. Why would anyone pass that up?

It would be very hard to discuss my first visions and thoughts without talking a little bit about the process of autopsies. When my dad was in the business, the function of picking up bodies and having the autopsies performed was outsourced to local funeral homes. In my dad's view, this provided a business opportunity that I discussed earlier.

The criteria for when the medical examiner would be involved in a death were pretty clear. It basically came down to a sudden death where some doctor would not be willing to sign a death certificate. (The death certificate was the official document that stated when you died and, more importantly, how you died.) This could have major implications on insurance payouts, as well as maintaining the dignity of the poor soul who was in attendance. Typically autopsies had to be performed on all accidents, murders, suicides, suspicious deaths, as well as deaths that occurred in a hospital if the person had been there less than twenty-four hours.

As you may have already suspected, the garden-variety suspicious death was not the one everyone really wanted to know about. It was the murders, suicides, and accidents that added some spice to my $20 fee. We were responsible for retrieving the body from the scene of the incident. This, in itself, often provided some of my more memorable moments. We had our share of plane crashes, car crashes, folks hanging, gunshots, and even a parachute that did not deploy properly, but the most popular by far were murders. Once we had picked up the person or persons, we would bring them back to the funeral home for the real dirty work.

It should be noted that the number of folks who attend your autopsy is a good indication of how unusual your death was or how popular you were. I have been to some autopsies that were truly standing room only. Everyone wants to say they witnessed the carving of someone who was either very well-known or found their demise in such a fashion that even the most hard-core detective had to be there. It would look good on the resume.

I always thought we should charge the folks that really did not have to be there. Depending on the situation, I'm sure I could have enhanced my $20 with some front-row seating as well as mezzanine and bleacher seats with binoculars. Cold beer would not be out of the question. It is interesting what folks think is a good experience and something to tell the grandkids about.

Anyway, once the body was back at the home, it would be removed from our black Plymouth Fury station wagon, lowered down the elevator, and slid from the stretcher to the aluminum table. The table was not cheap stuff. On four large rubber wheels, it could be moved easily about the room for various reasons. The lighting in this room was very bright. The table was slightly slanted so all fluids would drain to the bottom, where a one-inch hole could be found. There were gutters on the side of the table that moved the stream of fluid, usually blood, to the bottom of the table. As fluid reached the bottom, it would drain into a large sink. We also had a bucket on a hook if we needed to move away from the sink.

The body would be placed on the table, and a head block put under the head, which was used to prop up the head. Depending on the situation, the body might remain in the clothes that were on them when the event happened. An example would be a gunshot. The medical examiner would want the clothes in place to view entry angles, etc.

The doctors who performed the actual autopsies were usually regular MDs who had specialized in forensics. I'm not sure what they got paid, but I did always wonder what sort of doctor who had made a commitment to saving lives could be in this line of work. It seemed a bit odd.

The time would be scheduled for the autopsy usually very quickly. There were two types of autopsies: a "cavity" and a "full." The full included the head as well. That meant more time and that we had to pull out the special saw we had that was quite proficient at cutting through the skull bone without harming the tissue underneath. Generally speaking, the entire process would take about two hours. I have been to autopsies of murder cases that required much more time, some long enough that folks would have several cigarette breaks and even a pizza break if the time was appropriate.

In most cases these events were unemotional. Everyone was just doing their job. Raw language, jokes, and general horseplay were not uncommon. It was not meant in disrespect, but, I always believed, was intended to keep a rather morbid subject on the light side. If you do enough of these and see that frailty of the human body, not keeping it light could play havoc with your brain.

My dad would open the body with the usual Υ cut you see on *CSI* all the time now. Starting at each shoulder, an incision would be made angling toward the middle of the chest, then a single cut straight down to below the belly button. Once the cut was made, the skin would be peeled back to expose the rib cage.

There is no sound like the sound of that skin peeling back, the fibers ripping away from the bone. Of all the movies and shows on this subject that are around today, no one has captured that sound. I can only believe it is because they have never heard it. It is a missed opportunity in the horror show business.

There is really not a lot of blood for the most part, at least at this point. Next Dad would grab his trusty bone cutters. Think chicken wings. The rib cage would be removed using these incredible clippers. They were highly leveraged, allowing for a somewhat easy cut. Once the breastbones had been removed, the entire inside would be exposed. Lungs, heart, liver, intestines, etc. Keep in mind I am ten years old as this is happening!

Depending of the suspected cause of death, various organs were fully removed from the body cavity for further exploration. A good example would be a car crash victim. If the injuries did not appear to be sufficient to cause the death, the search was on. Did the person have a heart attack and then crash into the telephone pole? As discussed, if someone else has been injured or killed, you want to know the answer to that question. If they were drunk versus having a heart attack, the legal ramifications can be significant.

As the organs were removed, they would be cut in two to expose the tissue inside. To the trained eye, this can have all sorts of valuable information. A doctor who knows what he is doing can spot small blood clots, chronic diseases, hardening of the arteries, simply by observing the tissue up close. It may require that a sample be sent to the lab for further work, but in many cases it could be determined via the autopsy what you had died from.

The sight of a body cavity emptied of all its organs is quite unusual. Our body cavity holds some pretty large pieces of meat. The lungs, liver, and intestines to name a few. Seeing this spread all over the room can get even the most experienced, hardened lawman remembering his nachos from the night before. Of course, if someone did get physically sick, they would subject themselves to ridicule for some time to come. Mostly they would say they had to step out of the room to make a call, or some other sorry excuse.

When you see someone's innards spread out like this, it does give you a sense of awe concerning the human body and how we are actually intelligent thinking animals. Set up properly, it looks no different than the roadkill we all pass without noticing. An empty human cavity is one of the earlier sights I will not forget.

I mentioned the smell earlier. That smell was dead folks before they get to the funeral home. Once the work begins, there is still a danger in the air if you are not careful. It was not always that the intestines needed to be removed and investigated for an autopsy, but if it was necessary, great care was given so as to try not to "nick" them open. The instant that happens, everyone takes a step back and lights a cigar or cigarette. The smell that comes out of an open intestine can be very powerful. It does not matter if you had a fruit salad the night before or hot dogs and beer. I know folks who have the hot dogs and beer are accused of laying some nasty farts, but our fruit eaters have nothing to be proud of in this area. I have witnessed little old ladies that would knock you over if not properly prepared.

Having focused on the body cavity, it is now time to move to the head. Full autopsies that included the head were done on many cases that came to our home. The procedure would first include cutting with a scalpel through the skin from ear to ear, right above the forehead. A similar cut would be made in the back so that, in essence, the skin was not connected to the skull. Now the peeling again. The skin from the top of the head would be pulled forward so that it would cover most of the face, or at least down to the mouth area. If you can picture this, the top of the person's head, hair and all, are now in direct contact with their nose and eyes, exposing the skullcap. Of course, all bets are off if you happened to have died from a shotgun to the head, a baseball bat to the head, a telephone pole to the head—the list goes on.

I discussed car crashes earlier. I have removed folks from cars where their head has been crushed beyond recognition of anything that looks like a head. No roundness; just flat. Eyeballs popped out, and either nowhere to be found or not in the direct area. Although folks have said that the head can sustain a pretty good blow by a Nolan Ryan fastball and survive, some of the forces out there can be a bit overwhelming. Crushed heads or heads shot off result in some of the more unfamiliar sights one can see.

We've all seen the Halloween costume that is headless. This is nothing like that. The separation of head from the body is typically not a clean departure, although I did pick up a poor soul who was playing on the train tracks and stuck his head out between two stopped railroad cars at the wrong time. From the neck up was struck by a passing train traveling over 80 mph. It removed his head in about as clean a cut as I have ever witnessed. The problem was it took us quite a while and a long walk to fetch it back to its rightful owner.

Once the skin is peeled back, the special saw I mentioned earlier goes to work. It was pretty loud and emitted a smell as well that I will not forget. The smell of bone being cut with a high-speed saw it not very pleasant, but this thing was amazing. It would cut through the bone and never harm the brain tissue underneath. I'm not sure how they did it, or who they tested it on, but it worked very well.

Once the bone was cut through, the skullcap could be removed from the head. Another tearing sound that was not very pleasant, to expose the brain. The human brain looks just like you would expect. There was a famous Bugs Bunny episode when Bugs was captured in a laboratory. The mad scientist wanted to transplant the hare's brain into his Frankenstein-type character. The brain in that cartoon was just what the real brain looked like. When you consider that all our thought, feelings, perceptions, emotions, everything comes from this piece of meat, it really is incredible.

The Medical Examiner would look both inside and outside the brain. Of course looking inside a brain takes some initiative. Typically head posts were performed when the cause of death was not apparent from the body search that had just been completed. Once you slice into the brain, the brain no longer looks as interesting as it did from the outside. Spiced ham comes to mind, something I have not eaten in quite a few years. When you view an actual brain, it is hard to believe that it is an intelligent hunk of matter. Electricity swirling around. Childhood thoughts, biases, hatred, love, compassion, education, likes and dislikes all crammed into something that could be mistaken for a blob of something unknown. It really does make you wonder.

Anyway, once the autopsy was completed, the cause of death was either determined…or not. If found, the doctor would sign the death certificate, and the body could be released to the family. Actually it typically was released to the funeral home that the family had chosen.

This is where my dad had hoped that the traffic running through our place would result in not only the autopsy, but a few funerals. The idea worked, and Sullivan Funeral Home picked up more than a few $5,000 sales based on that early activity. It was a strategy I would later see play in almost all business models. Get the customer to the door then cross-sell them.

The pitch here was twofold. Folks who lived far away, especially out of state, would be embalmed before they traveled. It is easier to embalm a body while you are doing the autopsy versus closing the body up and having to reopen it all upon arrival. Many funeral directors would request my dad to do the embalming when he was done with the autopsy. Not a full fare, but certainly incremental income to the home. Many of these transactions were covered in cash or checks made out to him, which was nice for Dad.

If you want to get into a profitable business, think of the above model in Florida or some other place that is inundated with old folks who all want to be buried "back home." I know embalmers in these locations who only handle embalming and shipping the body. There is also paperwork that needs to be completed in the state in which you died. These guys make big bucks with very little overhead.

As an aside, I mentioned shipping of the body. Don't you know that the airline industry got into the act of profiting off the dead. They do not talk about it much, but not many flights go out that do not have someone flying down below where you are sitting. The next time you are complaining about flying coach, keep in mind there is another way to get back home that is even less comfortable and has no peanuts. The cost of these flights was never cheap. And, of course, they had a specialized shipping container that *had* to be used when transporting dead folks. As in *Weekend at Bernie's*, you may be better served just buying a coach seat for your "medicated" relative, and at least you can get the frequent flyer miles as well as two lunches if they happen to be serving. This poor soul could also have the always uncomfortable middle seat with no complaints.

The entire transportation part of death is big bucks. Hearse, limousines, flower cars, removals, shipping all add up. I'm not sure what the going rate is these days, but the thought of having a limousine to ride in during a funeral is almost borderline bazaar. Who are folks trying to impress? Certainly not the guy or girl in the box. You could be on a rickshaw or a bicycle built for two for all they care. As for hearses, that is truly taking advantage of the situation. I'm reminded of the scene in *Monty Python and the Holy Grail* when the man is going about town collecting dead people in a wheelbarrow. I'm not suggesting that we go that far, but certainly we can calm down and use automobiles more wisely when it comes funeral day.

I always felt that is one of those cross-sells that really tugs at your emotional side at the right time. A hearse and limo represent a dignified procession but really make no sense. Take your own car, rent a minivan for the casket, and give the money you save to HIV research or the Boy Scouts. Folks the day of the funeral may comment, but someone, somewhere, will be happier—someone alive!

Collectively, the thoughts and visions of some of the experiences I have shared are often bad enough for fully developed, mature men and women. As we grow older, we have experience with death. We see the news. We have relatives who pass away. We live through wars where death often can be minimized and become nothing more than a statistic.

I remember while we were in the funeral home, the Vietnam War was in full swing. On the daily news the reports would flow on about the many countless young men and women who had sacrificed for our freedom. Those reports, along with newspaper writings, pictures, and stories, do no justice to what death is really like. The physical aspect is something we choose not to address, as it is very unpleasant. The mental anguish that humans experience when a loved one dies can be overwhelming.

You often hear of folks who have been married for a very long time and one of them dies. It seems invariably, within a few years, the spouse dies as well. I have never seen a death certificate signed stating the cause of death as a broken heart, but I suspect it happens often.

The visions I witnessed, the realness of death, had an enormous impact on my well-being. A child should not be permitted near death or the funeral business until the time they are ready to deal with it. I'm not sure there is a set age, but it needs to be considered. In all likelihood, not many kids have had the experience

I am writing about, but if you, for some reason have an opportunity to keep your children away from death and dying, do so.

Do I feel like my innocence was lost? Absolutely. I do not think my dad did this with any malice, but it really fucked me up. It is no coincidence that around the time I started viewing this activity, I embarked on a drinking and drug career that spread over four decades. To this day I still deal with many thoughts and visions that no child should have to even imagine. I would ask that you even consider if young children should go to a loved grandfather's funeral. It serves no purpose and can have a lasting impression.

I realize I am an extreme case, but you never know when the line has been crossed. We need to protect our youth and immaturity, if that makes sense. Kids should be thinking about life, not death.

CHAPTER 6

JOHN LIST

I discussed that one aspect of having the county morgue was that we were called upon for many cases where the death itself was a spectacular event. Many of these stay in the news for a few days. Airplane crashes, multi-death events, and murders, to name few. You never know when they will happen, and you never know if they will be in your backyard so that you get access. It all is really the luck of the draw—or, if it's on the other side of the fence, the unluck of the draw.

The coroner often gets untethered access to some very secure locations and sights. If you are a police officer, EMS worker, fireman, doctor, or homicide detective, once your work is complete and you have been unsuccessful in your efforts to revive someone, you call the coroner. You really want nothing else to do with the cleanup and removal of the remains. That is where our role starts.

I have been given full access to some pretty tight locations over the years. Being a youngster made my presence at these scenes memorable for the authorities, and they often remembered me quite well. My dad had relationships with many of the doctors, cops, detectives, and so on, who were involved in the process, and his son was often with him. I walked under more yellow tape before the age of fifteen than Quincy did in his entire career. It is really amazing in retrospect.

The most famous death I was ever involved in is easy to recall. It is one that stayed in the headlines for many years and finally came to an end on *America's Most Wanted*, a long time after it happened. It really is important that I set the scene for this before we get started.

December 7, 1941, is a day that will live in infamy. Roosevelt said it, and it is no doubt true. Our country learned an important message that survived, some would argue, until September 11, 2001. Both events have many similar feelings and also cost many lives.

That day in 1941 was also another memorable day in the home. It was the day my mom and dad were married. On that day, as my parents emerged, taking their vows, word was spreading about an attack at a faraway place.

Of course Pearl Harbor's impact on America would drag us into a horrible war that impacted many lives. I could not imagine what it would have been like to have your wedding day interrupted by such an event. I imagine it could leave someone feeling robbed of the happiness and serenity of what should have been a wonderful event. Although my parents never spoke of that aspect of their wedding day, needless to say, December 7 became a date marked on the Sullivan calendar for years to come.

About seven weeks after their wedding, my dad enlisted in the Army Air Force, as it was known then, and became a tail gunner on B-29s, based on the small island of Tinian in the South Pacific. It was the same B-29 base from which the atomic attacks on Japan were launched.

He was honorably discharged in October 1945, after flying twenty-seven bombing missions over Japan. As was the case with many of that time, he did not spend much effort explaining his experiences. As for December 7, my parents not only remembered that "day of infamy," as most Americans do, but they also celebrated their wedding anniversary. This usually involved a house full of family and guests, and a party that often went on into the night.

On December 7, 1971, we were living in the funeral home. As was customary for the anniversary party, the usual assortment of scotch drinkers, beer customers, funeral associates, friends, and family were on hand.

I was fourteen years old and was a freshman at Holy Trinity High School in Westfield, New Jersey. The school was about ten miles away from where I grew up, and my freshman year was spent experiencing school and meeting a new assortment of friends at HTHS. Freshman year can be difficult enough, but going to school where I did not know many people had presented some challenges to my social skills. All in all it was going well, although I still spent time with the old gang of kids I had known from my hometown of Roselle. My friends from Holy Trinity would end up being a group of guys who, to this day, I still call my best friends.

I want to spend a few minutes talking about a quirk that my father had in the funeral home. I mentioned that he went to great lengths to acquire a "special" phone number for the funeral home. It was the one that would be published in the newspapers, phone book, and churches' weekly announcements.

The phone also had a special place in the home. When the phone in a funeral home rings, particularly at an off-hour, it means business. We had several phones around our apartment that were all strategically placed so that if, at any moment, some poor soul bought the farm, the home was there on two rings or less. My dad did not want to seem overanxious, but he did not miss a call. He would have to control his excitement, as the person on the other end really was not viewing the reason for their call as a revenue opportunity for the home.

When the phone rang—it had a special ring that was very loud—my dad would jump up out of his seat as if a fire alarm had sounded. He would literally sprint to the phone, catch his breath, and then put on his most sincere, caring, Father Flannigan voice: "Sullivan Funeral Home." This was in the days prior to called ID or other technological advances that could have helped set the tone for his call. If it had been a vendor calling and he knew it, it no doubt would have prevented him from getting all "Spencer Tracy" on every call.

Once the conversation on the phone began, I would be by his side, waiting to see what was about to transpire. Next to the phone he had all the support material he needed to "open" a case: a pen, a pad of legal paper, and an ashtray. Nothing else needed, thank you. Talk about minimal overhead. It is a wonderful sales model. No cold calling. The customers called us based on their heritage, religion, location, or some other obscure item that directed them to our home.

My father had a small wooden seat in front of the makeshift desk, which was really a dresser. The seat was the type that you see with a dining room. It matched nothing else in the room in color or design but was strong enough to hold my dad's two-hundred-pound frame when business was being done.

The first call we would get being notified of a death came in two flavors. When it was a family member of someone that intended to hold the funeral at the home, the call was of the very understanding type—name of the person calling and of the customer, address, phone number, when the person died, and where the remains were now. Based on when and where the person died, action would be taken to get the status of the body. Had it been released to the family? Treating doctor's name? All this assisted in getting the recently departed back to the home so our work could begin.

At the same time Dad would inquire who was going to be in charge of making the arrangements over the next several days. Dad would then arrange to either visit the home of the folks, or, if they chose, they could come to the home. He had a form that had to be filled out that would give him all the information needed to get the process started, kind of a checklist: death certificate, flowers, casket, vault, cemetery, visiting hours, mass cards, newspaper...on and on. It was like your final application. We spend our entire life filling out paperwork. Now, one more form to get you on your way out—one more form as far as we know. We do not know what lies ahead once we get to the pearly gates. It could be like the post office for all I know, lines and forms.

When these calls came in, especially after we first opened, they caused quite a stir in the house. Once my father hung up the phone, with a proud glow, he would announce the details of our new customer. If the candidate was still at home or in some other location and a doctor was going to release the body to the family, it was somewhat urgent that we loaded up the wagon and headed out for my $20 fee. If the customer was in the hospital, it was not as urgent. You still did not want to wait long in case someone changed their minds on the funeral home selection. Possession is 99 percent of a done deal. This scenario played out many times and was always cause to crack a cold beer, pat ourselves on the back, and say "job well done." Talk about someone's floor being another person's ceiling.

Again, this was a pretty unemotional event for the garden-variety death. Of course that was not always the case. If it was someone we knew, something unexpected, or strange or unusual circumstance, a detailed discussion would happen after the first call. "Uncle Joe finally bit the dust…I did not like him anyway."

The second variety of calls were the ones related to the coroner's office. These calls would typically come from a police officer or some other official who was involved in the death and dying business. This call was a lot less formal. "Hey, I got a good one for you…" When these calls came, it was usually something pretty exciting, but not always. These are the occasions where someone dies and the attending or primary doctor cannot sign a death certificate. They simply do not know why you died, and they request and advise that an autopsy be done.

There were also rare occasions where the family requested an autopsy, if they wanted more detail or if they disagreed with the doctors. In that case, the family would have to pay a fixed price. Often these calls started what could become us being on the inside of a big story or some unusual circumstance of a death.

Crime and accidents are the real interesting ones for most folks, and on December 7, 1971, at about 9:00 p.m., we got a call that would change the anniversary party that evening, my knowledge of Westfield, New Jersey, my perceptions of how horrible death could be, and my popularity in my new high school.

When the phone rang that evening, it was met with resentment. Someone was going to interfere with the party that was in full swing. This would not be the first time an event in our household would be interrupted due to the untimely death of someone we did not even know. Often my dad appreciated these calls, as he was not the type who enjoyed being around many people, so this was always a good way to get out of anything. After he got older he shared with me that he would often set his own pager off to get him out of situations he had no desire to be in. It is noticeable that the timing of death is really quite random. There may be statistics that tell otherwise, but for us it seemed like a roulette ball. Any time, any day, any place.

I was fourteen at the time. My role in the funeral business was at its peak—helping with the removal of bodies, general work around the home, and I'd even begun the real business of assisting with embalming and autopsies. Not many kids my age had that on their resume. I was bringing in a nice weekly salary, all cash that was being turned around into beer. Things were good. As I was unaware that my experiences in the home would prove to be a challenge down the road, it all seemed quite normal in some strange way.

In school I was the new kid from a relatively tough town, going to a Catholic high school out of town. Several guys from Roselle had also made the trip to Westfield to attend school, so early on I was hanging out with them, but as time went on, I began to make friends in my new town. Westfield was a middle-upper–class town that thought quite a bit of itself. Today, that is still true. They were very conscientious of looking their best and acting good, but in reality, dysfunctionality was the order of the day. My drug use and drinking really took off when I landed in that town. It seemed like the thing to do.

When the phone rang, my dad sprang to his feet and made his dash to the business phone located in his bedroom. I was close behind. When Dad reached the phone, he had no less that twelve Budweisers in him, but it was hard to tell. For him, twelve was just getting started. It was a cold, rainy night. The temperature was around thirty-two degrees, and the news had warned of black ice and possible sleet and snow moving in as it got deeper into the evening.

On the phone was Ralph. Ralph was an investigator for the Union County Medical Examiners Office. He was a good friend of my dad's. In a bit of irony, after working all of these cases,

Ralph himself was murdered by his own son over a drug issue in the home. Anyway, Ralph advised my dad that he had better get all resources on deck. There had been a discovery in the upscale town of Westfield. Four folks were found murdered in a home, and we needed to get to the scene with several cars.

My dad held up his hand with all four fingers held out. We had hit the grand slam. The murder victims were to be brought to our home! The ultimate in media exposure. My dad's marketing plan had peaked that night. We did not get much information on the crime at that time but were given the address.

Dad called a buddy of his who often did pickups for him and others in the area. Stash had a station wagon, and the plan was for him to head out to the address in Westfield. The thinking was that, between the two cars, we could fit all four folks. Stretchers were another concern.

As I mentioned, the funeral business has many products that are specific to the work at hand. The stretcher used by the funeral business was not dissimilar to the one used in the ambulance business. It could collapse down or lift up, and it stood about forty-two inches off the ground. Getting all four stretchers in the two station wagons was not going to be an easy task, but Dad was confident he could get it done.

Dad and myself jumped in the black Plymouth Fury and headed out on First Avenue, going west toward Cranford, and into Westfield. It was a ten-mile ride to downtown Westfield. Although I had started school in town, I was not familiar totally with the town and had no idea where the street we were looking for was.

It was around 11:00 p.m. when Dad pulled into the Westfield Police Department to get some information on what was going on and about the best way to get there. I waited in the car while Dad headed in. The rain was falling and beginning to freeze on the surface, causing a dangerous "black ice" situation. I recall being very excited about the trip, not knowing the details of what we were walking into but getting the sense that it was big news. I had no idea how big.

After coming out of police headquarters, Dad and I headed up Broad Street and made a right toward the upper-class side of an upper-class town. The north side of Westfield was filled with larger, older homes. Lots were large, and driveways were long. Well-manicured lawns with many large trees were all about. I imagined the pool service business was lucrative in this area.

The sleepy north side of Westfield, a commuter town to New York City, was going to wake to a shocking and, for them, unbelievable story that happened in this bucolic, "not-in-my-backyard" neighborhood. Ironically enough, after I had attended school in this town for several years, this neighborhood would be a place I frequented for many high school parties and drug purchases.

As we headed up and down the hills of North Westfield, we arrived at Hillside Avenue. Our new customers were waiting about six houses down on the left. The house was set back over two hundred feet from the road. It was an older house that stood out somewhat in that it had not been kept up as well as the others in the area. It was three stories high, an old Victorian that is common in these parts. The place was loaded with police cars, crime unit trucks, and other unmarked official-looking cars.

I mentioned earlier that you can tell how important you are by the number of folks who attend your autopsy. Another sure sign of popularity of either the person or the event is how many cops are on site. If there was ever a good night to commit a crime in Westfield, this was it. All resources were at the home of the John List family.

We parked on the street in front of the house for the long walk to the front porch. The freezing rain was building up, and it was slippery. This parking spot was not going to work when it was time to gather our customers up for the ride back to Roselle. We approached the porch and were greeted by several uniformed policemen. Dad always worked well with the police, and this led to some small talk about what was up inside.

A few moments later a gentleman from the Union County Prosecutor's Office who knew my father really well came out of the door. After greeting us, he advised the police we were cleared to come in and led us through the huge front door of the old house. To the right was a staircase, a large twisting staircase that looked like it came out of *Gone with the Wind*, solid dark wood with really nice trim work.

The ceilings were very high. On the left was a large opening to what was intended to be a living room that faced out to the street. This room was cluttered badly. Numerous metal filing cabinets were spread throughout the room. Papers were piled on top of them. It had the look of Oscar Madison's office from *The Odd Couple*.

There were several police officers still working in this room going through the piles of papers and folders that were on top of the cabinets. It all looked very out of place for the room, which was all dark wood. The detective explained that it was still a crime scene and we needed to be careful not to touch anything. There were cops all over the place.

Upstairs you could hear folks walking and talking. Flashlights were shining outside from detectives who were searching outside for evidence. The officer explained that, at this point, they were not totally positive the killer was not in the house or somewhere in the area. This was earning my $20!

I remember walking into the house. The front door was heavy wood. It was so cold I could see my breath. I walked around in the front foyer for the first few moments. My dad was chatting with the lead cops on the scene. I looked up at the fancy ceilings, noticed the dark woodwork. It really did not have the sense of what laid around the corner. I walked into the kitchen unattended. There was no one in the room but myself.

The room was riddled with bullet holes. Everywhere I looked there were holes. In the wood, the cabinets, the floor, the refrigerator. Everywhere. It looked as if someone went crazy and just sprayed the gun all over. There was no pattern to the holes. The other thing that stood out was the amount of blood on the floor, on the walls, all over the table. Lots and lots of blood. I remember standing there, thinking what this must have been like.

The kitchen was not large compared to the size of the house. In the middle of the kitchen was a pool of blood, with marks where a body had been dragged. The marks led out of the kitchen to the adjoining room. I followed the heavy train of blood into the room, where the List family lay in quiet, cold peace.

Adjacent to the living room was a room that was intended to be the library. It had no furniture in it. It was very large, with very high ceilings and large windows with nothing but shades. On the right-hand side of the room were several sleeping bags that were unzipped and stretched out. Laying across the sleeping bags were Patricia List, John Sr.'s loving wife; Patty List, age sixteen; Carol List, age fifteen; and John List Jr., age fourteen. All were laid perfectly next to one another, pointing in the same direction. Whoever killed them had taken the time to ensure they were laid together in a very linear fashion, the largest to the smallest.

All had a single gunshot wound to the head, except for John Jr. He had been shot so many times it was hard to tell exactly how many times. The kids were dressed in what appeared to be school clothes for folks of that age. Mom had a comfortable dress on. The house was very cold. The heat had been turned off, or else this could have been a real mess.

The detectives were not done with their work. Picture taking, fingerprinting, etc., were still in process. A few of the bodies were beginning, even in the cold, to rot. This typically starts around the stomach and the bowel area. There was minimal maggot activity. The killer was thoughtful enough to keep the place chilled, which prevented this from being a fly picnic.

We were instructed that it would be a while before we could take the List family back to our house. This rarely happened, but we now had several hours to wait, and we were inside one of the largest crime scenes in New Jersey history.

The first thing that happened was shortly after the wait began. An officer yelled from upstairs that they had found another victim. Victim number five. Alma List, his mother. Alma had been bound and shoved into a closet upstairs. She had duct tape wrapped around her and had a single gunshot wound right between the ears on her forehead. She was dressed in a nightgown. This raised fear around the house that there were more dead folks to be found. Police were crawling all over the place, both inside and out. I am fourteen years old and standing in the middle of this scene. The guys in school won't believe it!

No more bodies were found. The List murders were big news in suburban New Jersey. They would have been big news anywhere for that matter. That night, being in the place those murders took place, really made me think about what it must have been like in the few moments before you realize your own father, who as a child you learn to trust more than anyone, was on a killing spree, and you were about to die.

I thought of the son, John Jr., who clearly had put up quite a fight with his dad. He was shot sixteen times. Many wounds were in the arms, as if he were guarding himself from the onslaught of bullets coming his way. The terror. You are walking home from school, no doubt considering the day and what lies ahead for the night. Maybe dinner, homework, TV. You walk in the door. Did he sense that something was wrong?

John List was on the run for many years, living a new life, and was finally captured in suburban Virginia. Some visibility via *America's Most Wanted* prompted some phone calls, and the long arm of the law had its man. He was serving a life's sentence for five counts of first-degree murder. May he rot in hell!

I have never met John List but have become very familiar with the man—knew how he lived, how his children dressed, what their bedroom looked like, what was in their refrigerator, and what sort of toothpaste was in the house. I used his bathroom. John List has never thought of me, but our lives crossed each other's. He was not aware that a twelve-year-old boy would be picking up his dead family, nor did he know the impression it would leave on me for many years. I think about him from time to time and wonder if he ever thinks about the scenes I remember so vividly thirty-seven years later. I can almost smell the house and remember the ride to Westfield that night. Is it etched in his life as much as mine?

You see some crazy things in this business. The dose of morality that you are face to face with when you are viewing a man's wrath on his family is incredible.

We took the bodies back to Roselle as the sun was coming up. It was tight in the cooler that night, and the List family, sans John Sr., were quietly at rest at a comfortable thirty-eight degrees. We got some sleep, but the news was buzzing with what had happened. Pictures of the house we had just left. Reporters camped on the lawn of the large List spread in suburban Westfield.

The police and everyone else would be calling soon, and there was much work to be done. We had two autopsy tables, so we would have to rotate our customers as each autopsy was completed. It was going to be a long day. Remember earlier how I said you can tell how you lived and died by the number of folks who attend your autopsy. This was a sell-out—all the top detectives, police by the score, senior medical examiners, and, of course, me.

I do not have many vivid memories of the autopsies themselves. Garden-variety in some regards. I do remember John Jr. The theory was that he was one of the later kids to arrive home that day and had either seen something or sensed there was something amiss and was able to react and respond to the monster that was in the house. He apparently put up a fight with his dad and, in an effort to fend off gunshots, took sixteen direct hits in the arms, face, and torso.

I still think of the terror as you realize what is happening and that it is real, those few moments as the guns are aimed at you and firing. Then the frightful realization that it is your own father who is doing the shooting. John Jr. was about my age when he was killed. Mrs. List and her two additional children were apparently caught by surprise and shot a few times each in the head. It was unclear how the day had played out in terms of who was killed first or last.

One interesting aspect was the last victim, Alma List. Detectives chattered quite a bit about the fact that, not only had John slaughtered his own family, but he killed his mother as well. Some of the more seasoned detectives claimed they had seen plenty of families wiped out, but rarely does a guy kill his mom. Makes sense to me, but I'm not sure what the facts are on that.

Anyway, he not only included his mother in the carnage, but he was particularly brutal about it. Alma was an older, slight woman, most likely less than one hundred pounds. The kind of $20 pickups we like. The problem was that Alma was on the third floor, stuffed in a closet, hands bound with tape behind her back, and shot between the eyes. She was in her nightgown. When someone is stuffed in a closet for that period of time, they become frozen in the position they are in. Rigor mortis, they call it. She was as hard as concrete and rolled up in a little ball. It took a while to get the old gal flattened out, but after a while she was ready to go.

The theory on the List murders went like this: Due to financial difficulties, a father plans his family's execution in detail. The thinking that went into this plan was not done by a stupid person. Schools were contacted, the paperboy was advised, mail was held back. He thought of every detail, making sure he bought enough time to disappear in this vast land.

This is not intended to recall a murder that has been combed over in the detail by the media. John List's murders and his capture via *America's Most Wanted* have all had tedious coverage and recounting. This is more about my impressions of the night. At that age, I do not think we process this type of death the same as, perhaps, later in life.

Spending that night in the house became a real feather in my cap. Everyone in school wanted to know what it was like in the house that night. Many of the folks in my school lived in Westfield, so the story was really big news locally. Many friends had known the List kids from grade school and had good memories of them for the most part. Polite, into sports, not very wild. All would end up being shot by their own father very unexpectedly.

My impressions of the house itself were very vivid. The emptiness and disorganization of the house stood out. I wondered if this was how the house was arranged before they were killed, or did he do all the moving after the killings? Some rooms had little, if any, furniture. The room that four of the bodies were in had no furniture. Just the four sleeping bags spread out at the right side of the room, with the bodies of his wife and children on them.

There were large, nine-foot ceilings, which seemed higher due to the lack of furniture. Shades were on the windows. No other window dressing. The first room on the right when you entered the front door was crammed with filing cabinets, a desk, and office supplies. It appeared as if it had been dropped at the front door, dragged in the house, and there it had stayed. It was crammed with papers and files, and the police were had at work, reviewing every piece of paper.

It was here they found the note that was written to his pastor, explaining the financial misfortune that had befell him and that he found necessary to pass along to his family in a way unimaginable. The kitchen was a mess. This is where, the theory was, John Sr. confronted John Jr. They struggled, and the gunshots must have echoed in that house. Wood floors, no furniture.

I often imagined what those few moments were like. The room was riddled with bullet holes. In the refrigerator, the cabinets, the ceiling. The room was also covered in blood. There were also visible blood smears where the dead body was dragged from the kitchen to join his family members on the sleeping bags. Keep shooting until the fight is out of him. Dragging your own son by his feet in a pool of blood. What sort of person gets into that frame of mind? Can anyone who gets in financial straits have that ability?

For myself, I became associated with the List murders throughout high school. It would not be unusual for someone to introduce me and say, "He was in the List house that night." It fascinated the local community because of the nature of the crime but also because John List Sr. was nowhere to be found. His car was located at Newark Airport, Newark International Airport. Was I a post-witness to the perfect crime? No. John Sr. would show up many years later, living a quiet life in Virginia, playing gin rummy, and working at the local church. Two people in one. In jail for life, and now deceased.

CHAPTER 7

PLANES, TRAINS, AND AUTOMOBILES

Over the years in the funeral home, you see many things. Death does more than smack you in the face; it sleeps over. The death I saw at a very young age is not something anyone would recommend anyone should see. The raw footage that runs through my brain is not good. The thought of impending doom that results from years of witnessing these sights is tough to shake.

For my family, it was fairly routine. They had grown up in the funeral business for several generations, and the thought of working with dead people was not uncommon. Being a funeral director is one thing; taking on the county morgue duties is where I really got to see some shit. The mundane of the funeral business, although gruesome in itself, has nothing on the chore of cleaning up some of the more violent and unnatural deaths that can happen in this very human world we reside in.

When we read in the paper about some car wreck, we don't know what it really looks like. We see a smashed car and say, "Lucky if they are alive." When someone does not survive these wrecks, what is remaining can be truly horrifying. The human body does not hold up well when solids collide at a high rate of speed. All the air bags, side-door impact cushions, headrests, etc., cannot withstand the force of a vehicle hitting something like a big tree.

When I first considered adding a chapter about my most memorable wrecks, surprisingly a few of them were not hard to recall. After thirty-five years, you would think some of the details would fade, but that is not the case. The level of detail, _the smells_, the look in folks' eyes all come back too easy.

You need to keep in mind the setting here. It is the late '60s, early '70s, and things were different than today. Cars were not nearly as safe. They were high-powered and heavy. Big engines were what the youth of the day yelled for. Mustangs, Camaros, Firebirds. In addition to speed and power, the safety measures that are in place today are significantly improved—from the 55 mph speed limit to air bags. We have come a long way from the freewheeling days of yore.

Added to this was another key factor. It seemed like drinking and drugs were more prevalent. The combination of intoxicated drivers or drivers under the influence with powerful cars resulted in some crashes that really were amazing, not only for the shear power of them but for what was left in the wake.

We also seemed to have our share of older, larger cars that were involved in fatal collisions. Dad's old Chevy. If you ever have a moment, take a good look at a train, a real good look. This is not something you want to fuck around with. They are enormous, built of heavy metal, and they can go fast. That's all I really need to know. I have never seen a train that was damaged, no less disabled, by being in an accident with a car. Usually the train doesn't stop till the next town, even if they hit the brakes early. When you come to a train stop, wait and look. Believe me, it is worth the wait. I once picked up a guy off the Linden RR tracks that stuck his head out from a stopped train and was struck by a high-speed passing train at neck level. Cleaner than a razor, and the head was not found for miles.

This is a collection of more bazaar, strange, and terrifying things I have been paid $20 to pick up. Somehow I remember all these thirty-five years later too well.

PUPPY CHOW

Over the many deaths I have seen, one I still get a bit of a chuckle out of today is the following "tail"—no pun intended. It was an elderly gentleman who lived in a small Cape Code home. The home was well-kept, as they are for many older folks. He had a pet dog to keep him company. The dog was small and not capable of any damage from what we could tell. But things are not always what they seem.

The man died of what we found out later to be natural causes, but it did not appear that way at first. When the police were called to the scene by a concerned neighbor, they found this gentleman lying dead on this bedroom floor. His face appeared to be severely beaten. His nose was gone, ears missing. Lips and tongue nowhere to be found. It was hard to discern his facial structure. Most of the skin was missing from the area around his nose and eyes.

The police thought for sure they had a robbery gone bad. It was thought the man had resisted a robbery, was beaten, and was left to die. This was all until the gentleman's small and timid canine partner appeared from the basement. His face looked like he had just eaten a can of Campbell's tomato soup, covered in red. Crusted human blood and flesh stuck in his cute little doggy hair.

Upon closer examination, the police determined what had happened. The man had died of quite natural causes. Old age. The dog, left no food, became quite hungry and began to eat his master, one chomp at a time, starting with his face. I can only suspect that the master and his pooch were close, and dogs really do not appreciate what was going on, but if the police were not called and Fido had been left alone, we may have found nothing but a bunch of dog poop. Which was evident, by the way. Really makes you think about the circle of life.

Bottom line: closed casket. Dogs are great pets but have some natural tendencies we need to consider. If you feel yourself going, fill the dog bowl. Or buy a turtle.

UP A TREE

One evening a call came from the Rahway Police Department. Bad car accident on Inman Avenue, a typical two-way suburban New Jersey street lined with nice homes. It was fall, and the trees were bare of most of their leaves.

When we arrived it became clear this was a big event. Roads were blocked, and every cop in town was there. Special lights lit up the entire neighborhood like Shea Stadium. This road is not very curvy, but right at the spot where the kids lost control, there was a slight bend in the road. Four kids were driving at a very high speed, estimated later to be above 100 mph, and lost control of the car. They struck a very large tree. There were no skid marks—just a clean hit.

The car literally exploded into many pieces, as did its occupants. The scene was really chaotic when we got there, which was close to a full hour after the accident. That is faster than normal, but I guess there was no doubt about the condition of the passengers.

There were several poignant moments that I will find hard to forget. One was locating the driver's right leg, from the hip down, in the closed trunk of the car. How the fuck did that happen? Shoes, socks, pants up to the zipper. The part I recall was that the leg looked fake. No real damage. Just a leg. The trunk of the car was about fifty feet from point of impact. The rest of this kid was lying, ejected from the car, about one hundred feet up the road.

We were also missing one head, but not from the kid whose leg was missing. There was a young lady sitting in the passenger side, and her head was missing from the neck up. Not a clean cut either. Very ragged. We had the rest of a young girl, but this was causing everyone some issues. A missing head is not something we could leave the scene without! The police scanned the area with spotlights, and finally, with a pair of good eyes, one of the young officers yelled he might have located a head. About fifteen feet up, in a bare oak tree, was what appeared to be a pot of spaghetti and meatballs splashed on the tree bark. Think Spirto's. As we gathered around the base of the tree it was determined that, due to my slight build at the time, I would be a good candidate to get hoisted up the tree to get my $20 bucks.

As the Rahway PD held me steady, I went up a fire ladder to reach the grail of the evening. At eye level the scene looked much different. There was nothing noticeable as A head. It really did not look like anything human. I did see an eyeball, but it was not really attached to anything. They handed me up a plastic bag, and with one hand I began to peel the red blobs from the tree. There were some hard pieces. Skull, no doubt. This went on for about ten minutes, and it was determined I had earned my keep.

I climbed down and went back to work removing the rear seat passengers from the car's midsection, which was upside down on a front lawn with a big porch. The engine, fully intact had gone through the porch and was resting on its side at the bottom of the steps. These kids never knew what happened, but just a moment before, they were listening to tunes and having fun. That is the way it works.

Bottom line: Wow, I will never forget that day. The massacre that occurred in that car was incredible. I always wondered what song was on the radio in the car. Drive slowly!

THE PROFESSOR AND THE EGGPLANT

You do not always get time to prepare for death. Many deaths are very sudden, and, as such, folks can be found in some very compromising positions. It happens with hookers, druggies, etc. Everyone does shit they don't want *anyone* to know—until they die, and then they do not care.

We got a call to go to an apartment in Irvington, New Jersey—a high-level professor who lived in a big house in western Union County but maintained an apartment local to his college home to cut down on the commute and be close to the students. So far, so good.

The reason my $20 was there was to pull this guy out from a sudden death. He was a young professional. As it turns out, the professor was a wild man. He used the apartment for some crazy sex parties—S&M, whips, chains…the whole nine yards. This is no lie. This left-wing nut liked to suspend himself in a doorway with a contraption I had never seen before; it looked like some orthopedic equipment. He would then lower himself onto one of the many dildo-type devises he had, and this is how he got sexual pleasure.

Well, on this fateful day, the pickle beats the man. He was lowering himself down onto a really big eggplant. A special eggplant. The eggplant slipped—at point of penetration, slipped—and the professor fell and hung himself from the contraption. I'm sure the paper must have said he died suddenly. I do not know about that, but he had vegetables for his last meal.

Bottom line: open casket. Should have been closed. An interesting one. At the age of fifteen I realized that people will do *anything*. As for my job, it was really the typical pickup—other than my picking salad out of his ass.

You can see, I'm starting to earn my $20s. My point is that when you start your day, you never, *never* know how it is going to end. I'm sure very few people know how the good professor died, but make sure your undies are clean, as my mom used to say!

MY LUCKY DAY

This is a very sad story that I never forgot, even though I do not remember much detail about the kid's name, just a sad unlucky story that I witnessed.

Young kid driving on the Garden State Parkway northbound. It was about 3:00 a.m. at night, and he lost control and the car crashed. He fell asleep at the wheel. No drugs or drink. Young Jewish kid coming home from school. The car was in a terrible crash and finally ended up on its roof about one-half mile from the initial impact with a guardrail.

Of all miracles, the kid walked away from the demolished car—shaken up, but very alive. Drivers stopped, and the police arrived. The place was lit up like a circus, right by Galloping Hill Country Club in Kenilworth. The kid had been moved to the side of the road, and flares were set up, stretching out about one mile from the scene. It looked like the Fourth of July.

As the officer and the kid were discussing the situation, the driver realized he left his registration and paperwork in the glove compartment and asked if it was OK to get it. With police cars all over and the flares burning, the officer gave the OK. The kid walked over to his car and was bending down to get the paperwork (keep in mind, the car is upside down), and over the ridge came a drunk driver traveling about 80 mph. He plowed through the flares, just missing a police car, began a sideways slide, and hit the upside-down car with the kid bent over getting his paperwork.

I have thought about this one many times. I'm not sure that is the story that came out, but it is what the ME was told. I'm sure the cop on duty that night remembers the details even more than me.

Bottom line: closed casket. We are not cats. No nine lives. This really sucked. I cannot imagine.

WHO ARE YOU?

Early when we had the morgue, some of the attributes or drags of the job were not as glamorous as discussed. One chore was holding unclaimed bodies until someone stepped forward. It is really a sad state of affairs when you die and no one claims your body. No one.

We had the body of a black female, perhaps twenty years old. I remember her being very pretty. She remained unclaimed in our cooler for over five months before the state buried her as a Jane Doe. She became like a houseguest to the extent she was forcing Dad to keep the freezer low, which kept his electric bill high.

I always wondered who she was. How can someone just disappear and no one is looking? No one! She died of multiple stab wounds in the chest. The knife was large, and the cuts just as large. Who was her mother? Sisters? I recall that after twenty days she was so frozen it was like she was not real. She was just always there.

I felt a sense of disgust when we buried her. My dad and I did it alone at the cemetery for folks like this. There are sections, and they are bigger than you think. We did say a prayer together for her, but what a way to go. You would hope at least your enemies would be there.

Bottom line: potters field. Reality hit home again at a very young age for me. It seems very unfair. If you see someone who has no friends—they are easy to pick out from those who do—say hello...

EVERYBODY DOES IT

Tough subject coming up: People who are eating may want to put the book down. This is a tale of a poor gentleman who died a sad lonely death. There was nothing at all spectacular about his death. He lived above a bar in a tough neighborhood near the railroad tracks n Linden. The interesting thing about this ties back to a commonly understood (in the business) activity that happens when we die.

As you might imagine, when we die our body goes totally relaxed. All muscle control leaves the body. This invariably results in us humans pooping in our pants when we die. It is a rare occasion when we picked someone up who had not "shit" themselves, as my dad would say. It has a kind of twisted righteousness about it. All men and women. Rich man, poor man, beggar man, thief. Tuxedos, dresses, bathing suits, pants. It makes no difference how clean or sanitary you were your entire life. As one last physical act here on earth, we all let go one last load for our friends and family. It is the kind of thing only a funeral director would notice.

Here is how I learned that fact. One fine day we were called to pick up our customer at this local pub. No easy task. The guy was over three hundred pounds. No muscle. He also was upstairs in a narrow hallway. It was also a hot day. None of this was good. More importantly for my $20, the guy had really let a load go on his way out. It was really smelly and was all over the place. We noticed it was red, and there was speculation that the guy had some sort of internal bleeding due to his heavy drinking. Not being a pro at this, I was knee-deep in red shit.

After further questioning by the police, the bartender explained how our customer was a big drinker. All Bloody Marys. Morning, noon, and night. And I mean all the time. What we thought was blood was actually Bloody Mary mix. It was nasty. I smelled that for many weeks to come, but I did have a drink in that bar about ten years ago with my friend Pat, and the same folks were there. The stain was gone though.

Bottom line: There is some justice about this. I love the thought of Nancy Pelosi sitting in satin shit. But it will happen. I guess the dietitians are right.

LOOK OUT BELOW

It never ceases to amaze me how folks can find so many various ways to die. Many folks tempt fate by participating in thrill-seeking fun. When you see these on TV, they usually turn out alright. Even if something goes wrong, it seems they are interviewing the person afterward, and they are telling about their thrilling episode.

Of course all dares do not end up well. Today there are even more events that seem to push the limits of sanity. One of them, in my opinion, is skydiving. Skydiving seems like it may have had its start during wartime as a way to drop troops in behind enemy territory. Certainly noble. To jump out of an airplane for fun does not make sense to me. I know people who do this say it is exhilarating, being "one" with the wind. Bullshit. As my mom would say, if God wanted us to fly, he would have stuck a feather up our asses. I have seen one thing that many of those folks who enjoy that jump have not seen: what happens when the chute does not open.

One Saturday morning we received a call around 10:00 a.m. from the Linden Police. There was a small airport in town that has since become much more developed with more air traffic. At the time it primarily serviced private pilots who kept their small planes on the tarmac. There also was a school that gave skydiving lessons. For $35 they would take you up to about 7,500 feet and give you the privilege of jumping out of the plane.

Typically the folks who engaged in this activity were not first-time jumpers. They had repeated this insane act more than once. Well, our customer–to-be was a person who was quite an experienced jumper—certified, packing his own chute, pilot's license, the whole deal. Except this bright beautiful morning, something went very wrong. The chute did not open. He plunged at a very high speed to earth, splashing down on airport property. It was an amazing sight. This chap appeared to have landed feet first. He made a hole in the hard earth that was 10 inches deep. His legs were pushed so far into his torso that he appeared to be a munchkin from the land of OZ. The main, large bones in his legs were driven like spikes straight up through his body, destroying all his internal organs. By the way, for you safety nuts, his helmet worked as planned.

When we returned this young man to the home and proceeded to get his jump outfit off him, it was incredible how significant the damage was. The man was literally eight inches shorter than stated on his driver's license.

I have often thought about that fall. I'm not sure how long it takes a 180-pound person to fall 7,500 feet, but during that time, are you realizing that you are fucked? The fact that he tried to position his fall, feet first, always made me think that, till the very end, he was trying to get out of the situation. "Maybe if I land feet first?"

I'm sure skydiving can be fun to some folks, but I will never forget that one jump and the horrifying feeling for those few seconds. I'll leave the jumping to George Bush.

Bottom line: another one of those "people are fucked up" moments for me as a kid. I bet this stuff is fun, but I got to tell you, there has to be other stuff to do. My dad actually put this guy back together, and no one knew the better, although we did charge for a full-length casket even though we may have gotten a way with a child size. Remember, it's about the cash.

SEATBELTS, PRAISE RALPH NADER

I'm not certain how many lives seatbelts have really saved, how many injuries have been prevented. How many potential customers has this simple safety device kept from our doorstep? Millions in revenue.

I have, however, seen what can happen when you do not wear a seatbelt. Keep in mind most of my experience was in the 1970s. Seatbelts were just beginning to be recognized for their value. They were not in all cars, especially older models, and the shoulder harness aspect had yet to be enabled. They were primitive, but they worked.

I remember, as a teenager, it being somewhat nerdy if you wore your seatbelt. It's safe to say many teens felt the same way, so consequently, many of the wrecks I saw involved folks being ejected, partially ejected, parts of them ejected, or some other combination of the above. All were messy, but one in particular stands out for several reasons, as you will hear.

It was summer, and three teens were out cruising and having more than a few drinks. They struck a very large oak tree, full force, no brakes, at a very high speed. Interestingly, and contrary to my belief in belt usage, the two guys in the front had belts on. They were hurt, but their lives were spared.

The young man in the back seat was not as fortunate. He was sitting in the middle of the back seat. The front seats were bucket seats with a console in the middle. No seatbelt on. The force of the crash picked up this kid and flung him forward with such force that the front of his face was impaled in the front windshield from the inside. His head actually broke the glass and was stuck so that the crumbled glass outside was shaped like the boy's face. It was a creepy sight—his eyes wide open, mouth open, covered in blood, stuck in the glass. Inside the car, his body hung like a limp doll, the face supporting the entire body.

Once we reviewed the scene, the decision was made to begin to pull him from inside the car back into the car. It was not to be done. Two pretty big guys were tugging on his legs to no avail. Before I knew what happened, my father was standing on top of the wreck with a broomstick. He was smashing the glass around the guy's head to free him. It eventually worked, and his broken skull fell back into the car. The sight of my dad standing on top of that wreck with a broom and the guy's head hanging out the window was not easily forgotten. My point is that even if you are lucky enough to not be ejected, all may not turn out too well.

Bottom line: Buckle up, no matter the seat. I did wonder what the other two thought when they reviewed the scene. I bet that picture has stuck with them for a while.

MOTORCYCLES

This is another topic that, at minimum, deserves a mention. I'm not sure what the ratios were at the time, but we picked up our fair share of accidents where the victims were either drivers or passengers of a motorcycle. It could be the congestion of New

Jersey, being close to the highways, or the lack of protection motorcycles provide, but all these things combined have meant I've seen some pretty wicked stuff.

The one thing that really stands out are the skin burns that these folks have. The street tar itself is embedded into the skin. If there is skin. These burns can be everywhere and anywhere, including on the face. It can remove parts of the face in a second. Leg burns also are nasty and can be down to the bone.

As for protective gear and helmets, most of our customers were wearing some, if not all, the protection needed by law, and more. The point is, it really makes no difference when the right set of dynamics are in place—speed, nonmoving objects, etc.

We once picked up a young teenager on Route 1 in Linden. It was a busy intersection, and the kid and his bike apparently ran a light, and he was hit. He landed in the gutter on the side of the road. When we arrived, the highway was shut down and the red flares were in place. The kid was not that big, so Dad and I proceeded under the yellow tape with stretcher in tow.

A police officer standing next to the body suggested to Dad that we leave the helmet on or else we would be spending some time picking up the head that was in the helmet. Good enough for me. Helmet on, we took him back to the home for further examination.

Sure enough, when we got the helmet off, there was nothing left of his skull. It was like it exploded inside the helmet! His protective helmet! His brain was like small pieces of beef stew, with tomatoes pouring out of his safety helmet. His face was kind of there. The skin was not broken, but there were no solid pieces. What a mess.

Bottom line: My choice will remain four wheels. If anyone says they have all the safety gear there is, tell them, "Good luck. I'll drive."

WATCHUNG RESERVATION

We picked up a few folks up in this woodsy area west of Roselle and Westfield. It was a cool place to go when we were younger to hang out and do the usual kid stuff. It has a lake. Surprise Lake was small, but we did pick up a few drownings there over the years, usually drunk kids trying to make it across. Beer muscles.

At the top of the reservation's highest point was a large, tall water tower. I remember as a kid jumping the fence and climbing the stairs to the top. I was really scared.

Well, one evening we got a call that a man had been murdered in a house that was a few miles from the reservation. Dad and I headed up to this nice upscale part of central New Jersey. The murder was indeed interesting.

The father was sprawled out on the floor with a large ax sticking out of his head. Just like the movies, only the real deal. The ax was bloody, he was bloody, and, in fact, the entire room was bloodied. This was personal. I never forgot the look on his face, with that ax hanging there.

We began the process of getting this guy, with the ax, in place into the body bag. The ax had to stay where it was, in his head, for examining by the ME. It was literally sticking out of the stretcher's zip-up. Sometimes you wish you could get pulled over.

As we were loading our fellow in the car, the police received a report of another death that was located close by. Forty dollars on one trip! It was what appeared to be a suicide at the water tower a short distance from the sight where we were. This is a small quiet town, and the odds of these things not being related were low.

We went back to Roselle, dropped of the ax guy, and headed back to the reservation. Victim number two had made the 150-foot jump from the very top of the tower to the hard ground below. He hit headfirst. Young kid in his teens. It turned out he was the son of the guy with the ax in his head. This kid hit the ground with such force it knocked his shoes off. I'm sure there was a long tangled story there, or maybe not. I do know that Pat and I never really drank in the park like we used to.

Bottom line: Family ties are tough. You see things like this and say, "What the fuck could get folks to that state?" The crime scenes for these two were amazing. Very graphic due to the nature of the deaths. I could never have the balls to jump to my death from that height. Yowee.

CHAPTER 8

RANDOM OBSERVATIONS

As I look back on the many experiences I have had around dying and dead people, there are certain aspects of the entire experience that stand out—four memories, if you can call them that: (1) hospitals, (2) nursing homes, (3) deaths by fire, and (4) deaths by gun. Two are places folks go and end up dead, and two are ways folks get dead. Not proper grammar, but true.

In the first two, it is not my desire to belittle or demean the good people who work long hours as doctors and nurses in this country. Like teachers, they are the unsung heroes of this great land of ours. When you are alive. If possible, do not let a relative die in a hospital. Bring them home. It may be tougher for a while, but the hospital is in the business of saving folks, not tending to those not to be saved. When you die in a hospital, you become a piece of inventory that needs to be tracked till removed, and that is all.

Nursing homes, as they used to be called, are another location that, although I have very favorable memories of the folks who worked in the places, seemed very sad places. A sad location to die. Prop me up out on the beach when I'm ready. It's another place where they are not really built for hanging onto dead bodies.

I mentioned earlier that the rear doors in these places are usually not as glamorous as the front doors. Once you are no longer able to pay your tab at the hospital or nursing home, the back door has no flower shop.

I used to meet many interesting folks who worked in the morgues at the hospitals. Many folks were afraid to go the morgue, but there would always be one guy who would step up to the plate. It meant odd hours, no boss, and cash tips from funeral directors to lend a hand. Not a bad job if you can get past the content of the plastic body bags. They use the same kind in all hospitals—semi-clear plastic so that you could see just enough of the person, silver zipper, kind of a giant ziplock bag. Keeping freshness in and germs out.

It is odd the things I remember, like the body bags. When you work with something and see it enough, it becomes part of the routine, but since I left the business, I've noticed zero exposure to these items.

One side item regarding the body bags. I lived with my best friend, Pat, in an apartment in Garwood, New Jersey. We were living a college-type life in our own digs. We always had problems with the bathroom leaking. We were on the second floor, and the person underneath would complain that the water would come through her ceiling every time the shower was on. After careful consideration, we nailed a body bag that we cut open and enclosed the entire shower in body bag plastic. Never leaked again, but it did get attention amongst friends and family.

It would be interesting to understand where people want to die, once they grapple with the fact that they indeed do have to die. Firstly, you have the group of folks who die unexpectedly at an unexpected location. Always disruptive to anyone in the area.

You read about car wrecks and things like that, but the odder ones are when folks just die of natural causes doing something natural. Raking the yard and shoveling snow are two interesting ones. I have picked up more than one gallant snow mover. Let it melt. Another one that always had my attention was when someone dropped dead at a bar or eating establishment. Usually by the time we arrived, the crowd had thinned out, although I did pick up a guy at a bar in Linden, and several patrons remained at the bar drinking while one of them lay not fifteen feet away. Not totally as if nothing had happened, but not intimidated enough by the former patron residing on the floor in the rear entrance. A cold beer is a cold beer.

When I look at the obituaries today, I really look at the ages. There are certain groupings I have developed over the years, having categorized death in several different ways.

Under twenty years old: accident, drugs, suicide. All sad and not planned.

Twenty to thirty years old: an interesting mix. Seems inner city in many respects. Diseases that can be treated, but poverty has taken the opportunity for a cure away.

Over forty and into the fifties: seems to be the folks who live a hard life, either too much work or too much party.

Once you are in your sixties, no one can really say they are shocked if you pass on. That seems to be the point where people retire, don't know what to do, and die.

I also look at the really old folks. It seems like there are many little old black women who live to be over one hundred. It is tough to say what the right age to die is, but we all agree we want it to be as dignified as possible.

With that in mind, don't forget…your first few moments are spent with crap in your pants in a plastic bag. Tough start to your dignified trip to the beyond. I guess, from one perspective, funeral directors do clean up the mess that is left behind. An unpleasant job, but someone has to do it.

I mentioned death by fire as one method that seemed really to be a horrible way to go. We need to be careful. Many folks are burned but are dead before they're burnt. This is often the case in house fires, where the smoke gets you before the flames. I'm talking about folks who die as the result of being burned in a fire. You see these souls who survive and are scarred and disfigured for life. Dying in a fire must be a horrible and painful way to die. Many of the bodies I picked up in fires were huddled, as if they were trying to protect themselves from the flames, often in closets covered with a blanket or under a bed. Their arms were often clinging to themselves. Those last few moments as the heat rises, too hot to breathe, and then you are unconscious.

I have seen bodies burnt beyond recognition. This usually is when dental records or some other form of DNA is used to ID who the person is. Some are easy to get at based on the car they were driving or the home they lived in. Others are more difficult, such as airline crashes where you have multiple deaths.

When you are young, it is very difficult to make any determination about the line of work your dad or family was in at the time. I say "at the time" because, as you get older, you can make more sense of events that have occurred in your childhood. Many of the scenes I described in this book happened at a very formative time in my young life.

I know now that I, in the past, struggled with the decision to let my daughters even attend a funeral when they were younger. When you think about a twelve-year-old kid with his hands in a body cavity up to his elbows, the discussion is "how much damage did it do?" to this child, not *if* there was any damage.

But that was not the way this was viewed in my house. I was simply working in the family business. The funeral business had been in the Sullivan family tree for three generations. Working in and around dead people was not as weird to me as it may have been to other kids my age.

I do not recall the first time I actually laid eyes on a dead person. It had to have been at my grandfather's workplace, and I was likely between four and six years old. I recall from time to time going to the funeral home with my grandfather, but not a lot of dead body stuff, and I do not recall being scared. Seems odd now. By the time we opened the funeral home in 1966, I was about age ten. At that age, I had been exposed to some very difficult visual pictures. Not too many ten-year-olds have such a real image of death and dying. The face of mortality as seen through the eyes of a youngster.

It may not have been much of a coincidence, but around the same time this exposure started, I also began to drink and use drugs. As mentioned on many occasions, drinking played a big part in the old-time funeral business. It also did not hurt that both my parents were raging alcoholics. I was growing up in the '60s: My parents drank, my friends drank, and I may have wanted to block out what I saw inside the funeral home.

Whatever the reason, I went on for thirty-eight years, allowing alcohol and drugs to cover the hidden fears I had. Many of these fears centered on dead people. I saw friends who were still alive in situations I recalled from the past. I obsessed about dying, always afraid in every situation because I had seen death in every situation. I knew how vulnerable the human body was. At a time when most kids think they can beat the world...I knew they could get run over and killed. I saw it.

I'm not sure if this experience and perspective has been harmful in every aspect, although I suspect it has done more harm than good. My doctors tell me that the exposure I had may have, indeed, contributed to some aspects of what rolled out in my life.

Now, as I pass the fifty-year-old mark, I still think about what happens to you when you die. Not the physical aspect. That I have seen enough of. What happens to our spirit after our physical being ceases to live? Does it just end, that simply and easily? Could be.

At this stage of my life, I find that belief or faith in a higher power makes life easier. I pray for the families who have to live through some of the real-life horror that can happen to each and every one of us.

Most of the people died a very fast death. No time to think. Is that different than the person who has to spend months dying of cancer?

I have often thought of how different my perspective of death is from the majority of the population. As a youngster, our thoughts of invincibility often fuel some of our more daring and fun adventures. I was no exception. Driving fast, drinking, and drugging—all were activities whose consequences I had witnessed firsthand. In looking back, it did not seem to concern me that we had customers who died a result of the same activity in which I was participating. Perhaps, due to some hidden guilt, it seemed to accelerate my addictive behavior. Perhaps it was to block out harsh memories or dismiss having any feelings at all.

I know, over the years, my obsession with death and dying was not healthy. Death, as a topic in general, because of its nature, still has many unanswered questions. The human aspect that we lightly touch on in this book is really not the important part of death. I think that natural curiosity is what the afterlife is about, and I relate that to the carnage and sorrow we see around us, and it is a lifetime mission.

With the help of much therapy, I have been able to put much of what I witnessed behind me. I no longer start the morning off by reading the obituaries. My dreams have subsided significantly, and other than the daily eccentric behavior, things are moving along.

Death is not a funny subject. Ever.

When I look back on all of the terrifying scenes that crossed my path, it is hard to believe it actually happened. Now that is it over thirty-five years ago, some of these thoughts seem very far in the distance. It still amazes me the detail of events that I can recall simply by trying to remember certain things.

Sometimes something totally unrelated will remind me of an event that happened in the funeral home. I was recently driving down Route 1 in Linden, New Jersey, and death and dying and this book were really not on my mind at all. I was stopped at a red light, and I looked to my right to find the Swan Motel.

I'm sure many folks can recall a good story from the Swan. It was the type of place you really would not be staying in unless you had to. The instant I saw the name, I recalled a visit my dad and I had there over thirty years ago. A traveling salesman who was staying at the motel found his demise when somehow the room he was staying in ignited in a very large fireball. The inside of the room was burned to a crisp. Nothing was left. The heat must have been tremendous. The salesman was burned beyond recognition. I recall picking him up, and his skin simply falling off the bone like an overcooked chicken. The smell of burnt flesh is something you will never forget. His limbs were like burnt fat on the edge of a steak.

I recall it took a good hour to collect all the burnt pieces and put them in our "to go" bag. Sitting at that light for just a few moments, thirty years later, it all came back as if it were yesterday: the smell, the search for next of kin—which, in this case, was no easy task—and, finally, the car the gentleman had.

All traveling salesmen have cars, and this guy had a brand-new Ford LTD GT with a 400 CI engine. The car was sweet. The reason the car came into play is that we eventually found the guy's family. They were estranged, and no one had any interest in re-trieving him, no less his car. My dad cut a deal that we would bury the guy in exchange for the car. Done deal. This poor bas-tard got blown up, and the Sullivans get a slick set of wheels out of the deal. Barter for funerals. Not a bad idea.

The reason I bring this up is not so much the story about the guy and his car, although there is a lesson to be learned there. The striking thing for me is how these stories can come out of the blue. They are all just sitting there, waiting to be triggered by something.

The irony is that what I took away from the exposure to all of this death and dying was much more subtle than the headlines that interest the average folk. Most people will die very quiet, un-noticed deaths. I do not mean that in the sense of the closest rel-ative, but in the sense of how it impacts the total population.

On the other hand, something extraordinary at your death can make up for a lifetime of failure. It doesn't matter if folks do it quickly—such as a suicide—or if they take the longer ap-proach—stress, addiction, the list goes on. Or it could go the other way, and folks just break down, kill a bunch of people and themselves. Death has many options and opportunities.

What impacted me most and what I remember the most were the garden-variety deaths. That is the one most of us will experi-ence. You get over fifty, the age we all should begin to really worry. From there on, no one should be shocked about any po-tential outcome. How we die, what we are doing, and what it tells folks about us.

I have come to the point where there is not one thing anyone can tell me that I do not consider possible. When it came to catching folks in the middle of dying, taking them back to the home, we were on the front line of what people do when they only expect to get caught if they die! I'm confident the guy with the large vegetable up his ass had no thought of getting caught and being the talk of the Union County Police for a few weeks to come—no less the mention in this book. He assumed that the in-sertion would be discreet.

When you die, discretion becomes hard to control, at least from your perspective. Not only that, but the entire time from when you die onward is really for those who are left behind. The two to four days—one if you are Jewish—really need to be redirected.

The guy who dies working on the dock, the nurse on the run at work, the truck driver who pulls over, the heart attacks mowing the lawn and shoveling snow. The old folks over seventy-five. Some die at home sitting in their chair. I personally always like that one. Others keep active and are doing something they should not be doing, like diving. I have picked up my fair share of victims at the hands of blind, deaf seniors demanding to keep their driving privileges. They kill themselves often and do harm to others just as often.

Paging back, I'm not sure how much the average person today is exposed to death and what happens after you die. What they do with your remains, the cost of a funeral, the add-ons you can have. I know that, since I have left the funeral business, I have not been to many funeral homes. I guess that makes some sense. It was a creepy business to be close to, and in retrospect, is not something a child should be exposed to.

GUNS

No story about the funeral business and our coroners' activities would be complete without a dedicated mention of guns. I have never fired a gun at anyone, but I sure have seen the results of folks who have had the unfortunate experience of having a gun aimed at them.

Gunshot wounds can vary widely. I remember more than one occurrence where we had to search hard to find the gunshot point of entry. A small caliber gun makes a very small entry wound that can be hard to find if it is in the hairline or in an odd place on the victim. On the other hand, a large caliber gun or a shotgun leave no doubt what was hit and where it went. It seemed to me that many of the folks that we picked up were shot at close range, usually some sort of dispute.

John List Jr. was a gunshot victim I will not forget. John, it was theorized, was the last of the List family to be executed. It was also believed that when he entered the house, he sensed something was amiss and was tentative. Either way, his father unleashed a barrage of shots at the kid in an attempt to stop his resistance. Although the fatal shots were to the torso and head, John Jr. was shot more than sixteen times in the attempt to stop the rampage. Many of the shots were in his arms. I always visualized him covering up as the shots continued. It had to be a furious few moments echoing in that empty house.

I was always transfixed by folks who had the misfortune of being shot in the head. It seems like more than one person was the victim of a shotgun blast from close range that landed in the head or upper torso. It is a favorite shot of thugs during robberies. The damage it does is unbelievable. Even as you are staring directly at the victim, it does not register. When Dirty Harry said his magnum would blow your head off, he was not joking.

These cases are clearly closed caskets. They do make for a difficult embalming, as many of the vessels have been disrupted and you can spend some time trying to get all the pieces back together. No need for makeup or hair styling for these folks. Simply do your best on the reconstruction, wrap the body up in plastic, and lock the lid.

The other popular gunshot wound we would see was suicides. It's curious that someone would choose to shoot themselves versus using a softer way. I have seen instances where folks have built some pretty elaborate contraptions to get a rifle to fire a bullet into their head. It is not easy to reach a trigger on a rifle while the barrel is in your mouth.

Suicides often draw an interesting crowd to a funeral. I must say, of all the various ways people die, the crowds that show up at the funeral of someone who has taken their own life are by far the most somber. Not sure if it is guilt, or just a lack of what to say, but there is a very strange aura around someone who takes the final leap on their own. The normal chatter around a funeral is how the person died. Old or young, this will be topic of discussion at all of our funerals. At a suicide, that topic is off limits, and it leaves folks with a void in the social aspect of the event.

As you might expect from the funeral director's seat, a suicide is akin to "pulling business forward" in corporate America. Nothing different, except the timing of the transactions. Funeral directors need to be discreet with these types of deaths. Families are often very tentative about discussing how their next-of-kin dies if it is a gunshot. It seems natural, but the details are really never brought up or discussed.

Usually at the funeral, some relative would step into my dad's office; it always seemed like an uncle of the corpse. They would tell Dad the real story. "Little Larry has been fucked up since he was kid; this is no surprise. We are just glad he didn't kill us as well."

So much for guns. I have seen a lot of damage done with guns up close. I now have a real aversion to guns. I'm not sure if it is directly related to my experiences, but my observations are that guns leave a wake of damage that is never good.

FIRE

As discussed earlier, if you work on or around dead people, you are aware of what a body that has been burned looks like and, more importantly, what it smells like. I hated picking up bodies that were burned. It is a sight, sound, and smell you will never forget.

There are several varieties of deaths that can be caused by fire. The old adage that most folks die from smoke inhalation before they burn is of very little comfort to the guy picking up the remains. The ones I clearly remember were in automobiles. A car wreck takes on an entirely different set of circumstances if fire has been introduced. Folks get pinned in the car, the car catches fire, and the rest is history. It cannot be a very pleasant last few moments. I have removed folks from cars who were still sitting in the driver's seat and were burned beyond recognition, their clothes and hair burnt off.

You often hear the term "burned beyond recognition." What exactly does that mean? In laymen's terms, think unattended barbeque grill. The black hot dog at the back of the grill after a big party.

Burnt flesh has an unbelievable smell to it. It cannot be mistaken for anything else on this earth. You can get an early hint of it if you ever have the opportunity to burn your hair. Take that smell times ten. We would get very little assistance from the EMS and police in the area when we were picking up one of these customers. It is no fun. The skin is slippery and can at times fall off the bones like an overcooked spare rib. When that starts, you can end up with several bags of "extras" that will be taken along with the main torso, all to be reviewed back at the home.

It had been my experience that very few people actually died from the flames. Usually the smoke got them before the flames. If you have ever seen anyone who has suffocated from smoke, it can be very ugly. A black phlegm oozes from the mouth. During the autopsy, when you open the person's body cavity up, you can actually smell the smoke inside the body. The lungs will be seared like tuna.

I have always thought that death by fire (not smoke) has to be the worst, but I've also concluded I would rather be cremated than rot in the ground. The big advantage with cremation is that you can stay behind—the mantle, the trophy shelf, or just hanging on the coffee table. I'll always be there! I kind of like that.

Cremation seems to be getting more popular these days, certainly more popular than it was in the 1960s. I always feared the thought of being buried underground. Not that you are alive, but just the thought is creepy. Of course, being a bowl of ashes does not leave many options either. Something about those ashes sitting in the home of loved ones feels better than sitting in the cold field of St. Gertrude's.

One final thought: My dad had a customer who requested a cremation for his wife. No service, just pick up and cremate. Low budget. He would come by to pick up the urn at a later date. Well, he never came back, and I suspect till this day those ashes are still where my dad left them. We would use that urn as a sales sample if folks were asking about cremation. Little did they know it was filled!

HOSPITALS

I mentioned hospitals early on. When you are in the funeral business, you get to know hospitals very well. It seems dying at home is not as popular as it used to be. Either you are in the hospital and die, or you are about to die and they take you to the hospital. When you read that someone was pronounced "dead at the scene," that usually means the damage was so extensive that the emergency personnel did not attempt to get to the hospital.

It always felt like hospitals were made to die in. They had all the necessary things needed to handle a death. I never want to die in a hospital. Although it seems like the place to be when you are sick, as soon as you die, the hospital really cannot do anything else. That results in your value as a customer taking a drop. Now you are simply taking up space. You know the old adage: You were a prospect then, now you are a customer.

We had several large hospitals in our area, Rahway and Overlook to name two. Due to our regular visits, we would get to know the folks who worked in the morgue at the hospital. The people who take morgue duty at a hospital are often an interesting group. Over the years, I noticed most were older versus younger. That makes sense. They often were folks who had a very philosophical approach to death. You would often hear that the reason they took the duty was they did not have to listen to customer complaints as they did in other areas of the facility.

The duty of those folks was pretty light when you consider we did all the lifting. They basically would let you in, make sure the toe tag was the right one, sign out, and lock up. Simply system, but it worked. I do not recall us ever getting back to the home with the wrong customer.

The other advantage, from a pickup perspective, when you remove a body from the hospital is that it is usually cleaned up a bit and in a good quality body bag. Body bags are key to an easy removal. Just as it made taking out the garbage easier, these plastic bags have helped in keeping many a customer in one place.

Body bags are on of the many items used in the funeral business that go unnoticed. It is the windshield wiper of dead bodies. It makes everything easier. A good quality bag is not cheap, and since every baby boomer in the world is going to purchase one at some point in the next thirty years, guaranteed, it may be a good investment.

I mentioned that it seemed fewer and fewer folks die "at home." I'm not sure if that is true, but when someone dies at home, it is interesting. Your home is really not made to have a dead person in it. I remember my Aunt Mary calling my dad to tell him Uncle George was watching TV and she could not wake him up. Dad and I zoomed over and, sure enough, Uncle George had watched his last baseball game. He was sitting in his normal chair, beer and peanuts by his side. Now that's planning. He looked very natural sitting there.

When a dead body is in the house, it is noticeable. Sometimes folks react differently. We were called to a bar in Linden one sunny afternoon to pick up someone who had collapsed while dining. When we got to the scene, our customer was laid out in a hallway returning from the men's room. The thing I found interesting was that there were about six or eight guys sitting at the bar about fifteen feet away, having beers and watching the game. Two guys were playing a bowling game nearby. I guess death affects everyone differently, but these gentlemen did not see this as a reason to disrupt the afternoon.

NURSING HOMES

They do not call these places nursing homes anymore, but no matter, they are still a primary source of customers. In the '70s it did not seem like there were nearly as many of these places as you see today. They are everywhere now. There may be more of them, but they still seem like very depressing places.

The customers we would get from these places were very old and under one hundred pounds in most instances. The folks in nursing homes seem to have much more empathy for the dying than those in the hospital. I guess it is the nature of the beast.

My dad did have a good idea regarding nursing homes that should have stuck, but I am not sure it did. After every funeral, instead of taking the flowers to the cemetery where they would be left to rot, I would deliver them to the local nursing homes, where the folks there would put them around the place. I can tell you that these flowers put a smile on the faces of the folks in the home, when they were truly intended to be a sympathy offering for a dead person. Seems like a good use of resources.

CLOSE THE LID

When I reflect on my younger days, I was certainly in a unique situation, having witnessed things that the normal child would not have seen. Not many kids could say they spent the night in John List's house when the bodies were discovered. I used John Lists toilet paper! Can your teen say he picked up one of the victims—a young teenaged girl found in Roselle—of the recently (suspected) deceased serial killer, John Zaransky? Climbing under that yellow tape allowed me into a world that was really not intended to be viewed by children. Did anything come out of this besides a severe case of PTSD? Some thoughts...

- I certainly have had a good appreciation of driving fast and what it can do.
- I think I unconsciously lowered the bar for myself by witnessing how fucked up some people really live. I'm cynical in that regard.
- I realize people die in some really crazy ways (think vegetables page 62).
- I fear riding motorcycles.
- I don't care for tractor trailers on the highway.
- Many people die very lonely. More than you think. They are not in the obituaries, so we don't see them.
- I learned about empathy. Losing a loved one can be extremely upsetting and life changing.
- It's taboo to talk about it, but we have a crazy way to honor the dead.
- Embalming fluid can be a quality high if used properly (not recommended).
- The funeral industry has a vulnerable customer base. Be aware.
- Brains do look like the ones in Bugs Bunny.
- Autopsies are gross, even if you are used to seeing them.
- Anyone who dies under the age of 30...it is the saddest.
- Little kids are the worst deaths, no matter the cause.

- Most doctors are arrogant when not around their patients.
- The technology of toe tags has not changed in decades.
- Folks who sell funeral supplies make lots of money. It's an under-the-radar industry.
- I like that Wal-Mart sells caskets now. We are heading in the right direction.
- Some folks, although not many, look scared when they die. Most just look dead.
- Your mouth is always, always open when you die, and you drool. You cannot stop it, so do not worry about it. It's expected.
- People overspend on the pageantry of a funeral. It has a holiday feel to it sometimes.
- Squished people are gross, especially if their head is flattened by something.
- Stay away from guns.
- Embalming machines are very interesting. How do they test them?
- I wonder if florists make more money on Valentine's Day or working the funeral crowds. I bet I know.
- I wonder if churches make more money on baptisms or funerals? I bet I know that one too.
- Baby boomers will make this a growth industry for years to come. Opportunity is knocking.
- Are funeral homes excluded from Angie's List?
- Bagpipes should be required at all funerals. They are the perfect sound for death. Leave it to the Irish and the Scots.
- Parachuting is unnecessary.
- Seatbelts are good. No exceptions.

I hope you have enjoyed this view of a subject that is not discussed often. I have tried to cover some of the scenes I recall from my youth and how what I saw affected me. I really set out to recall some of the more peculiar ways folks have died. It is important we keep in mind that the backdrop to this book was over thirty years ago. My cage was rattled a bit recently with the deaths of John List and John Zaransky, both of whom crossed my path in a strange sort of way. But most of the folks are memories not nearly as well known. That is how most people pass through this world. It may be the ultimate lesson in humility.

How this impacted me as a young person is hard to measure. As a general rule, now I keep young kids away from death and dying. There is a concept they need to grasp, but by no means should a young kid be exposed to some of the graphic and bizarre things I had the chance to witness. If I had had my way, I would have stayed a kid for a few more years. I do believe, because of this experience, I have developed a unique awareness of things around me and the frailty of life itself.

It is important we all come to accept death as a natural way of things, but that is the spiritual side. The physical side has been filled with man-made problems and solutions.

Please visit my Web site and tell me your stories about funerals, death, and dying.

EPILOGUE

Where did the idea to call the book *Switching Heads* come from?

When folks asked me what I was going to call this book, the answer was easy. "Switching heads" was an old line I learned in the business at a very early age. Working in the home, we often had to move dead folks around. From the stretcher to the embalming table, embalming table to the casket, casket to the viewing room. In case you haven't noticed, dead folks do not co-operate when you try to move them, hence the saying, "like trying to move dead weight."

Sometimes people would show up for the viewing and not like the suit or dress that their loved one was laid out in. Wrong color, too low cut, hated the suit, etc. This would involve us having to "change" our customer in the hour between visiting. Not an easy task. It would be at this point that my dad would say it might be easier if we just switch heads. No one would know the better. As long as it is your dear relative's head, do you really care that it may not be the rest of them? You never really saw the other parts of them anyway, and it would make our job much easier.

I tell the story of how we would switch heads on bodies when circumstances or timing did not allow for a more complete transition. The look I get from folks was the thing that convinced me that folks really do know nothing about their final trip to the beyond.

Everyone's first reaction is, "They do not really do that...do they?" I usually confirm that, not only are heads switched, but all sorts of parts can be moved much quicker using this method. Kind of a real life Mr. Potato Head.

Do they really switch heads? Take a look next time and see what you think.